READER REVIEWS

Niall Cluley - Global HR Director, Fitness First Group

A perfect 'go to' source of inspiration on how to present playing to your own style and strengths! I have known and worked with Chris for the last 15 years following his impressive journey developing as an expert in the field of leadership and organisational development. Building on his highly successful corporate energy programme, this book is packed full of practical and thought provoking ideas that can help any leader, manager, trainer or aspiring public speaker with their presentations and audience engagement.

Lee Smith, Editor in Chief, Journal of Internal Communication

This is a rare book, one that gets beyond the theory of employee engagement and actually delivers genuinely useful and actionable lessons all of us can benefit from at work. Chris has distilled decades of experience into book which doesn't just deepen our understanding of how to engage employees, but provides practical and actionable advice on how to make it happen. If you want to inject energy into your workplace, this is a great place to start.

Debbie Clifford - Director of Learning, Talent & Performance at The Brinks Company

This is a fantastic resource and toolkit for anyone who currently presents or needs to present ANYTHING. It is a very insightful look at why we are sometimes not as effective as we want to be as well as being full of handy tips, hints and tricks to make a much more impactful communication style. Not only food for thought but also sustenance to keep us growing and improving.

Bill Fox - Global HR Director at Innovia Films

People are what drive an organisation. Great companies ensure that they develop a culture of true engagement, whereby when walking through the factory gate or office door, people feel inspired AND empowered to contribute to their maximum ability using all of their skills sets and expertise. What is key to this is the alignment of people, achieved through ultra-clear, effective and authentic communication. In this book Chris captures so many of the components that make communications work. In a practical way he describes how to optimise each and every opportunity you have to communicate with your teams to ensure understanding and alignment. In turn that creates the positive Corporate Energy needed to drive true engagement. This is a really useful book and one that can be referred to again and again. Keep it close by!

Huw Lewis MBE - Managing Director of Motivational Preparation College for Training

Corporate Energy should become a field book for EVERY inspiring executive who wants to connect and communicate a company vision and their values in an effective, professional and motivational manner. As a Managing Director for a company with staff spread over the entire UK, I have worked extremely hard over the last 17 years to engage, motivate and educate my staff to achieve the company cause. Therefore, when I was given the opportunity to read Chris Atkinson's book Corporate Energy, I was delighted to have the chance to learn about the skills and techniques to inspire individuals and groups to be their very best. This book not only talks directly to its audience but also has the depth of knowledge to create a positive impact immediately.

Professor Steven West - Vice-Chancellor of Bristol UWE

In the words of Simon Cowell, "I don't like it...I love it!" Once in a blue moon a book comes across my desk which really does engage me. This book is engaging, informative and above all makes you question and think about what you are doing and how you might be perceived by others as you do it! It's a great blend of practical solutions and approaches supported by case studies and resources. It's a guide to be dipped in and out of. It would appeal to new leaders and managers as well as some seasoned, old battled scarred leaders, looking to refresh and rethink their approaches. Something for everyone!

Edda Björgvinsdóttir - International Speaker, Actress, Comedian, Writer and Director

This book is amazing! Wow - now at last I have something to back up what I am trying to teach all speakers. You capture the facts in very simple and very understandable sentences. I loved it!

Christele Canard – Founder, Switched On Leadership Magazine

An insightful and comprehensive guide to help you inspire, engage and connect with your audience. From structuring your presentation for impact, to using technology effectively, Chris Atkinson has got it covered. Filled with practical tips and techniques to not only energise your speech, but also your audience. This book is a must-read for those wanting to stand out and make an impact.

Paul Tuck – Former Global Head of Talent, Zurich Insurance Group

This is a great read. It is informative, not just as a 'how to' manual full of detail on communicating with impact, but also as a 'why to' guide to understanding the reasons for engaging your people. Chris has managed to strike the right tone for first time presentation tips whilst providing a great refresher for the more experienced communicator – a reminder to stay alert and engage with your audience in order to inspire them.

Rod MacKinnon - Headmaster of Bristol Grammar School

Far and away THE most accessible, complete and authoritative guide to effective communication I have seen. Packed full of practical guidance, referencing academic research and a wealth of first-hand experience, Chris Atkinson's book reassures, as it educates, as it inspires. We are reminded of what we partially know but have lacked the understanding to appreciate fully. We are also introduced to new appreciations of the power of communication and how it works. I enjoyed this brilliantly clear, complete and accessible guide to communicating to best effect.

ABOUT THE AUTHOR

Chris is an international business speaker and author who combines a strong commercial approach with a deep understanding of human psychology.

He has qualifications in the fields of psychology and counselling from the University of Bristol, UK.

Starting his speaking career in 2001, Chris has now worked with diverse business sectors in over 20 countries worldwide with more than 40 different nationalities. He has spoken in front of an estimated 30,000 people worldwide.

He is renowned as a speaker, master trainer and facilitator who specialises in audience engagement, organisational culture and inspiring leadership.

Chris has been featured on the front covers of international publications *Realizing Leadership Magazine* and *Switched On Leadership Magazine*. He has a regular column in Business Leader Magazine. He has also written numerous magazine articles with a readership covering the UK, Europe, North America and Australia. He is also visiting fellow at the business school at the University of South Wales.

CORPORATE ENERGY

HOW TO ENGAGE AND INSPIRE AUDIENCES

CHRIS ATKINSON

Published by New Leadership Press, 2016.

Illustrations by Kate Tuck

ISBN 978-1-911079-41-5

NEW LEADERSHIP PRESS

CONTENTS

CHAPTER 4: Facilitation Skills

CHAPTER 5: Inspiring Others

CHAPTER 6: Handling Questions & Disruptions

CHAPTER 7: Using 'Technology'

A message from the author

Fundamentally, this is a book about how to communicate. Communication is not just an enabler for engagement and inspiration, it is the very key to unlocking it. Communication is the lifeblood of organisations, and without it there will be no life, no energy, no engagement and, ultimately, no organisation.

Research has demonstrated how bottom line results are significantly improved through engagement, and the important role communication plays in promoting this engagement. This may be through leaders and managers or through the wider communication within the organisation. This book is packed full of practical ideas, tools and techniques designed to generate energy, inspiration and enthusiasm in others. But these tools are simply the vehicles; your personal passion, courage and commitment are vital to achieving the results you desire. You are 'subject number one' in this grand experiment and your first challenge is to lead by example and embody the enthusiasm you hope to see in others!

As the book progresses, the skills discussed become more advanced and challenging to master. I begin with the focus on you, the communicator, and move deeper and deeper into how to connect with your audience. It works as a strategic narrative, building up layers of argument and explanation to help you develop a greater understanding of human psychology and communication. For this reason, I would recommend that you first read the book from start to finish in order to gain the maximum benefit. Then, whenever you are facing a specific challenge, you can use it as a quick reference aid, dipping into the relevant sections for guidance and inspiration.

To inspire and engage others is a great challenge, and at times incredibly hard work, but the rewards are huge. It is the highest skill of leadership. There are very few other things in organisational life which feel as good as seeing the people around you 'light up' about a subject as they engage with your content.

I wish you huge success,

INTRODUCTION

A sad truth about why this book exists:

Culturally most organisations lack energy, life and vibrancy
...But you can change that

Cast your mind back over the last few meetings you attended. Consider how these meetings were structured, how it felt to be a participant, how passionate the meeting leader was about the topic(s), how engaging the content was. Now consider this: what did you do differently as a result of those meetings? What changed in your world?

Maybe your answers are mixed, but I suspect not.

In the majority of meetings you have attended, you have probably sat and listened to commercial/corporate updates, looked at dates and figures and left having taken very little of value from that time. Your behaviour is unlikely to have changed as a result of your participation in that meeting; likewise, your attitude towards the topics covered. So how do you feel about your work? Does it motivate and inspire you? Do you enjoy what you do?

It is wonderful if you are one of the fortunate people who gets a strong sense of satisfaction and purpose from their working life. But if you do, you are certainly in the minority.

We know employee engagement is a critical issue for organisations and it is one that has significant financial implications. Consider the research: Aon Hewitt's ***2015 Trends in Global Engagement*** included a massive 6.7 million employees and represented more than 2,900 organisations. They found organisations with high levels of engagement "outperform the average company on revenue growth (6 percentage points), operating margin (4 percentage points) and total shareholder return (6 percentage points)."

Conversely "Bottom quartile engagement companies perform worse than average on all financial indicators."[1]

Deloitte University's ***Human Capital Trends 2015*** report is one of the largest longitudinal studies of talent, leadership and HR challenges around the world. The research involved more than 3,300 business and HR leaders from 106 countries. The report stated "employee engagement and culture issues exploded onto the scene, rising to become the No. 1 challenge around the world in our study. An overwhelming 87 percent of respondents believe the issue is 'important,' with 50 percent citing the problem as 'very important.'"[2]

All of this paints both an urgent and challenging picture for organisations. Our working lives are becoming dull and soulless, which is sucking the joy and vibrancy from our workforce. More specifically, the challenge sits with leaders, managers, trainers and executives whose responsibility it is to engage and motivate employees. These people are privileged; they have the opportunity to present their ideas in an interesting and inspiring way and to invite a passionate response from their listeners. But here we face a critical problem: for many people, the idea of standing in front of a group as a presenter, facilitator, trainer or leader is a very uncomfortable prospect. This discomfort makes people act in a more introverted way, preventing any possibility of engagement and inspiration.

> *The human brain starts working the moment you are born and never stops until you stand up to speak in public.* **George Jessel**

Fortunately, being ingenious creatures, we discovered a wonderful way to avoid this discomfort.

PANIC
WE FOUND A WAY TO AVOID BEING THE CENTRE OF ATTENTION...
UMM...
WE FOUND A WAY TO STOP WORRYING ABOUT WHAT WE WANTED TO SAY...
P
...WE FOUND POWERPOINT! (OTHER SOFTWARE AVAILABLE)

For these reasons, presentation slides have become the cultural norm for communication even though most people readily acknowledge the negative impact they have on engagement. In fact, there have been concerns about PowerPoint's effectiveness since the earliest days of the software. In August 2003, the Columbia Accident Investigation Board at NASA released Volume 1 of its report on the crash of the space shuttle Columbia. The report cited an unexpected culprit: the board argued NASA had become too reliant on presenting complex information via PowerPoint. "When NASA engineers assessed possible wing damage during the mission, they presented the findings in a confusing PowerPoint slide...so crammed with nested bullet points and irregular short forms that it was nearly impossible to untangle."[3]

In 2010, the New York Times published an article referencing the negative impact of PowerPoint within the American Military, called ***We Have Met the Enemy and He is PowerPoint.***[4] In it Gen. James N Mattis of the Marine Corps, the Joint Forces commander, is quoted saying at a conference, "*PowerPoint makes us stupid.*" At the same conference, Brig. Gen. H R McMaster, who banned PowerPoint presentations, likened PowerPoint to an internal threat. The article concludes, *"Behind all the PowerPoint jokes are serious concerns that the program stifles discussion, critical thinking and thoughtful decision-making."*

One of the most outspoken critics of PowerPoint is Edward Tufte, professor emeritus of political science, computer science and statistics, and graphic design at Yale. He uses the analogy of a drug: *"Imagine a widely used and expensive prescription drug that promised to make us beautiful but didn't. Instead the drug had frequent, serious side effects: It induced stupidity, turned everyone into bores, wasted time, and degraded the quality and credibility of communication. These side effects would rightly lead to a worldwide product recall."*[5]

We can't expect software and slides to engage or inspire. If anything, technology is likely to hamper your efforts to engage. For many, less experienced presenters it is a *challenge to overcome* rather than a tool to enhance. Technology can't deliver inspiration, nor can it engage, because these are emotional responses. The thing that stands the very best chance of eliciting either of these responses...is YOU!

Look around you. Our organisations are dying because we haven't invested in culture. We've failed to prioritise the experience of work and the spirit of our organisations. Without a culture your organisation is meaningless; it is simply work for cash, and that type of organisation will not survive. The organisations that are thriving in today's market are animated by their culture; their leaders inspire and engage through creative, meaningful communication.

You might assume that there are a lot of training programmes and information resources focussing on *how* to engage and inspire. Unfortunately, the opposite is true. There is certainly a lot of material designed *to inspire you,* but little to none on the critical *how* question. Consequently, people who have mastered this skill are watched with admiration and a certain degree of wonder. Others may try to replicate or mimic their style but mimicry will not work because, crucially, it lacks authenticity and becomes merely acting. Real mastery of the skill requires a strong foundation of knowledge and a genuine passion.

After repeatedly hearing people say they'd like to be more inspirational or more charismatic, I realised this issue has never really been addressed within organisations. Many people in today's workforce are frustrated by the lack of effective communication, and they *want* to do better themselves. We have a highly educated and increasingly open-minded workforce. People *want* to be engaging and inspirational, they actually *care*! But there are no programmes they can follow, there are very few books, and there is the common assumption that you've either 'got it, or you ain't'. This simply isn't true. These are skills you *can* learn, and I'm going to show you how. Learning the art of successful and engaging communication is hugely rewarding, both for you and for your audience.

It is truly staggering that there aren't more resources available. Mark Crowley in his book, ***Lead From The Heart,***[6] concludes: "*According to a seemingly endless number of research studies - all arriving at the same conclusion - the workplace has become profoundly destructive to the human spirit.*"[7] This book addresses this loss of 'spirit' and provides practical, valuable tools for re-energising your organisation. Whether you are leading or facilitating meetings, workshops or training sessions, it will help you develop the skills to present your information in a way that motivates, engages and inspires.

> "*No matter how great your product or service is, no one will hear about it if you don't attract attention - it's that simple.*
>
> **Richard Branson**

For references and links from this chapter visit chris-atkinson.co.uk/books

CHAPTER 1

STRUCTURING TALKS & PRESENTATIONS

Before you start working with a group you will (hopefully) get the opportunity to plan and prepare. Preparation is crucial but it often gets squeezed into a short period of time. Worse still, most of that time is usually taken up putting slides together, often with little consideration for the communication techniques, strategic narrative or the presentation style. Give yourself the very best chance of success by taking time to plan. For an important presentation we might set aside a day or more, but even a short presentation should have a dedicated planning period.

1.1 What is my purpose?

The first step in structuring an effective presentation is determining its exact purpose. You must be clear about the subject of the presentation *and* its purpose - they are not the same thing! Frequently the purpose is set by someone else, often with a brief that is vague or without specific aims. This will inevitably lead to disaster. Do not hesitate to question and clarify the purpose of the presentation prior to accepting a brief. If you are setting the brief yourself, allow time to clarify in your own mind what you are looking to achieve.

Here are some ideas and recommendations:

To Influence or Persuade

You wish to convince the audience about an idea or outcome

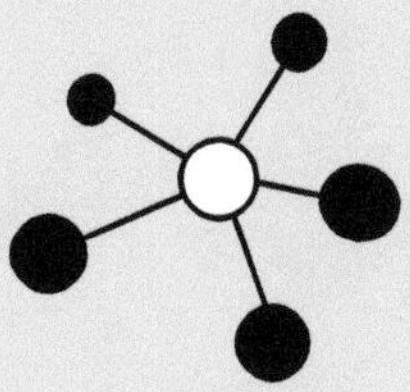

- Start by emphasising the problem
- Use facts and evidence to illustrate
- Suggest a number of possible options
- Make a clear recommendation, with evidence

To Educate

You understand something which your audience may not fully understand

- Start with simple terms and build up the complexity
- Use clear and concise language
- Use visuals to simplify complex ideas
- Provide hard copy reference materials

To Inform

You need to make the audience aware of important information

- Narrow your presentation down to a few key bullet points
- Be very clear about what the audience are expected to do as a result
- Allow time for questions

To Entertain

In one sense every presentation should entertain. Your aim is to make the audience glad they were there and glad you were the presenter

- Tell light hearted stories of your failures and what you learnt from those experiences
- Experiment with showmanship to make your presentation memorable
- Be bigger than normal! Talk more loudly and use bigger gestures - don't worry, you will not look as 'over the top' as you feel

To Motivate

You need to energise the audience about a subject, idea or a change

- Give examples and illustrations
- Paint a bright picture of the future
- Focus on the gain and benefits
- Address the possible concerns

> *Purpose is the guiding light that illuminates a path through the dark and tangled forest of content – it enables us to select, arrange and shape our material meaningfully.* **Martin Shovel**[8]

1.2 Know your audience

It is as difficult to meet the unknown expectations of an audience as it is to hit an unseen target. Yes, it's *possible,* but it's a risky way to seek success. If you truly want to engage and inspire then part of the process of preparation should be dedicated to gathering information about the audience.

Some of the things you should consider are:

Knowledge and expertise

Experience

Prejudices

Needs and wants

Key goals

Speakers often assume that, because they feel passionate about a subject, their audience will feel the same way and share their passion. This a common trap for presenters. You must consider the **WIIFM factor**. WIIFM is the dominant psychology for all audiences you address; if you don't understand it you will likely fail to engage. WIIFM stands for: '**What's in it for me?**'

To exaggerate the point slightly - the audience doesn't care what you are talking about, they care how it affects them. Most often, when a presenter starts talking about their subject the audience will lose interest very quickly because the speaker hasn't considered its significance to them or framed the content of the speech accordingly.

Column 1. Speaker Cares About	Column 2. Audience Cares About
Health and safety	My personal safety Why is it an important or relevant use of my time? What happens if I don't?
This month's results	My bonus My workload What do I need to focus on?
New process, system or restructure	Fear for my job Concern over my current skillset Why are we doing it?
Induction or orientation information	Where do I go when I have a problem? When do I get paid, and how? Who do I need to know in the organisation?

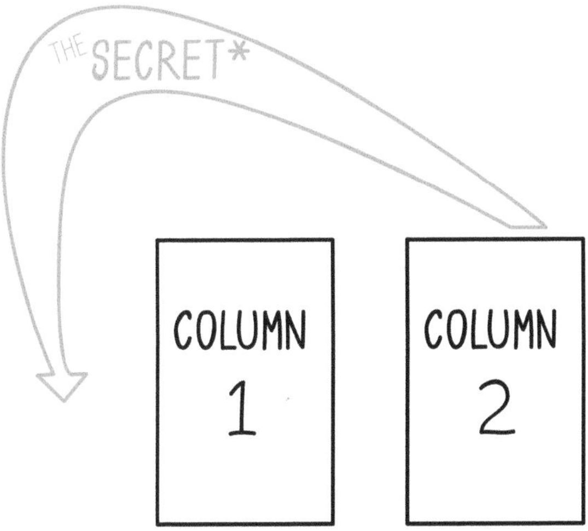

As you read through the table you might feel that your presentation addresses all these issues. My challenge to you is *when* do you address these issues? My guess is that you begin by talking about the subjects in column 1 and then move on to column 2. The secret to success is to simply flip this around!

For example:

> *"Welcome to today's session on health and safety. Today we'll be discussing the latest government guidelines on personal protection equipment which affects most areas of the site. We'll also look at the changes in the law and some things you need to be aware of when you are working in the different areas of the site. Let's start by looking at the recent legislation changes..."*

By starting with column 1 information you probably feel that this is important and relevant, but sadly your audience will have already started to disengage. Now imagine if, instead of this introduction, you started with column 2:

> *"Welcome to today's session on health and safety. You're probably wondering if this session is going to waste your time, and how much of the content will be relevant to you. Well, the behaviours we will speak about in the next hour are about keeping you safe, not about being pedantic. Imagine the impact on you and your family if something were to happen to you. Moreover, failing to follow the correct procedures could lead to immediate disciplinary action and could leave you exposed to legal prosecution, which is something none of us wants..."*

In this second example you are speaking directly into the questions, interests and even potential cynicism of the audience. The direct approach grabs their attention and tells them you understand their world. Of course, once you have their initial interest you must explain *how* these important changes will be achieved, and at that time you will need to move to column 1.

So, be very careful about making assumptions. It doesn't follow that because something is important to you, your audience will share that interest. You must take time to understand the attitude, interests and concerns of your audience. This is the language that you should use from the outset. If you are uncertain about your audience, do some research, take time to speak to some of them, run an online survey, or talk to others who have worked with that group.

1.3 One structure to rule them all

There is a surprising amount written about how to structure presentations[9] [10] [11]. In an attempt to engage their audience, many people (wrongly) assume that the solution can be found in the right structure. Whilst having the right structure is certainly very important, ultimately *you* have the greatest impact on how much an audience engages. Your priority is yourself; your style and your delivery.

That said, the structure you choose can make your life easier or harder. The most well-known presentation structure is: Tell them what you are going to tell them, and then tell them, and then tell them what you have told them. This is actually a reasonable principle and a good starting point, but I will go one better.

There is one structure whose simplicity belies its potency and effectiveness. This structure can form the basic template to create powerful presentations. I call this the OMEC model:

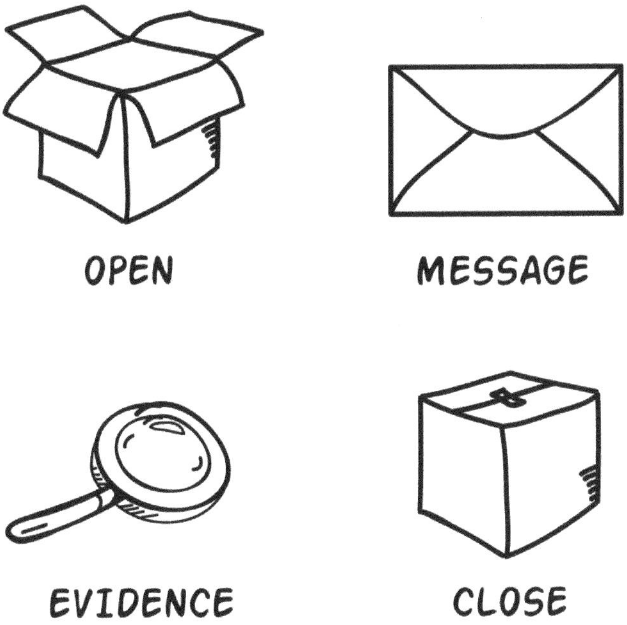

Perhaps you think this structure seems rather obvious. If we look a little deeper into the theory behind it, we can see how the vast majority of mistakes made by presenters can be seen in this structure. In addition, when done correctly, a few tips and tricks can ensure the structure also provides a significant ‘wow factor’.

The opening serves two important purposes:

1. Grab the attention of the audience (first impression)
2. Set the agenda, context, timings etc.

Have the courage to start with the attention grabber BEFORE your name, the agenda etc.

3

This is the key thing you want to say to the audience

Most presenters make the disastrous mistake here of following their passion for the subject. Your message needs to be simple and easy to understand; the more you talk the more your message will be lost!

Keep it SHORT and SIMPLE

Refine your message down to just one or two sentences.

1

This is the proof of the claim you make in your message

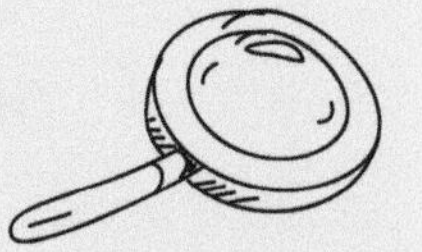

Since you are already convinced about your message, it is a common mistake to assume that the facts are self-evident and require minimal evidence to back them up. Evidence is vital. Types of evidence you might consider include: facts, statistics, personal experiences, demonstrations and exhibits.

Make it as LONG and as COMPLEX as needed, always considering the level of the audience's understanding.

2

Summary of the key points and a call to action

It is important that the call to action is absolutely concrete – be specific about what you expect your audience to do as a result of your presentation.

Connect your closing to whatever you said in your opening statement, and you will impress your audience!

4

One of the most important and fundamental rules when preparing your presentation is:

Don't ever start preparing by opening PowerPoint!

If you use presentation software to prepare your presentation, it is a sure-fire road to boredom for your audience. The reason is simple:

You open the software and create your first slide – a title slide

Then you create a second slide – this one has your agenda

Then another slide – this one has information about you, or housekeeping

Then another slide – this one has the first thing you want to say

Then another slide – this one has the next thing you want to say

Very soon you will find you have **A LOT OF SLIDES** because you are using your slide deck as a scripting tool. In the example above you may only be a few minutes into your presentation but you already have 5 slides. We will discuss presentation software in much more detail in chapter 7, but the concept of 'death by PowerPoint' is well established and this is the primary reason why slides can be so tedious for your audience.

I propose a far simpler and significantly more effective approach. Did you spot the numbers in the OMEC model table? My recommended approach is this; take a pen and paper and prepare your presentation in the order shown. In other words:

1) Write down the **message** you want the audience to hear - remember, just one or two sentences.

2) Make a note of a selection of **evidence** that you believe would most powerfully influence the audience.

3) Think of an attention-grabbing and impactful **opening** (see section 1.5 for a detailed discussion about openings).

4) Finally plan the action you will ask the audience to take, and link your **closing** to your opening statement.

Now, having noted the outline of your talk, consider:

5) What visual aids and slides can I use to simplify my message or illustrate my points?

You will most likely find that you create far fewer slides and that those slides have significantly less content. You will also notice I've said visual aids as well as slides. There are many interesting ways of creating visual support for your presentation, slides are just one form. The greater the variety of media you use the more memorable your presentation will be.

Visit the chapter 1 resource page of the website to see a short video of the author speaking about Leadership Communication

1.4 The primacy and recency effect

The two simple psychological principles known as primacy and recency[12] were discovered early in the 20th century by Hermann Ebbinghaus[13]. They were extensively studied during the early years of the field of psychology, but were slowly forgotten over time. Today you will find very few people who know and understand these two words, yet we now take for granted the truth of their meaning.

Primacy – *We remember the first information we are presented with better than later information. It is believed that this information goes into* ***long term memory*** *efficiently, whereas later information doesn't get stored as easily.*

Recency – *We remember exceptionally well the final few pieces of information we are presented. It is believed that this is due to the function of* ***short term memory*** *which can hold a few pieces of recently presented information.*

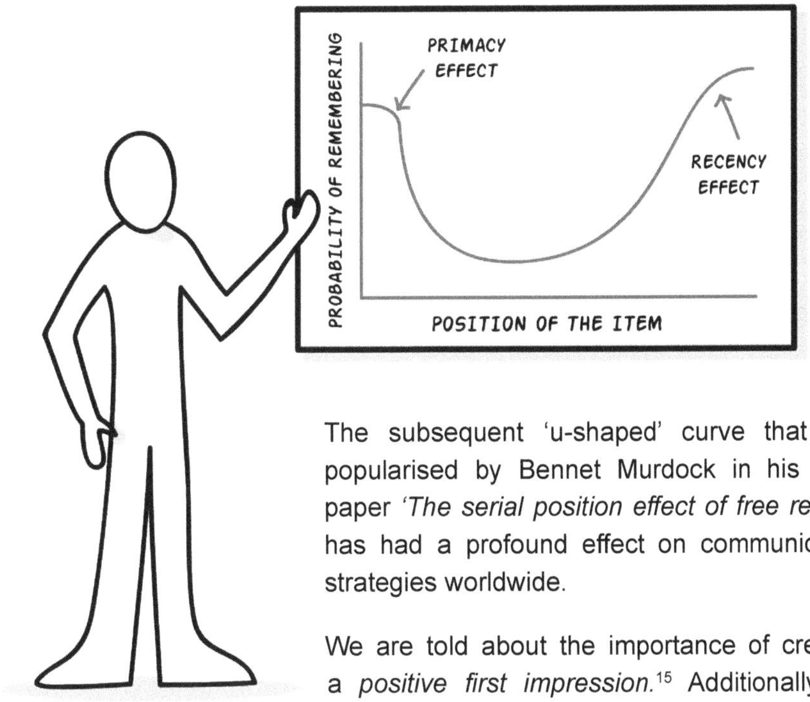

The subsequent 'u-shaped' curve that was popularised by Bennet Murdock in his 1962 paper *'The serial position effect of free recall'*[14] has had a profound effect on communication strategies worldwide.

We are told about the importance of creating a *positive first impression.*[15] Additionally, we are told to leave people with a message they will remember. This is simply the primacy and recency effects in operation. Marketing experts use this methodology to sell products: they ensure that the first message you hear about a product/service is positive, and that the last message you hear encourages you to take action (in this case 'to buy').

If you ask an airline pilot about the skills needed to be a great pilot, they will tell you that the two most critical moments in flight are take-off and landing. These moments require great concentration, focus and practice to perform effectively. It is the same with presentations: your take-off (opening) and landing (closing) are critical. Unfortunately, human psychology works against you:

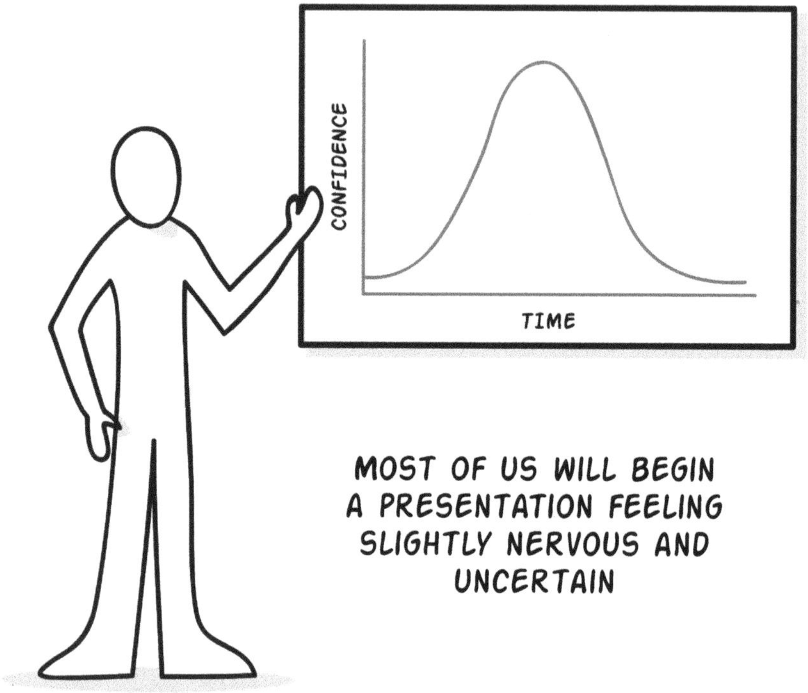
CONFIDENCE
TIME
MOST OF US WILL BEGIN A PRESENTATION FEELING SLIGHTLY NERVOUS AND UNCERTAIN

Slowly we'll find our rhythm and confidence, building up to a good level of comfort mid-way through our presentation. We are aware of the importance of a good, strong ending, but as we draw towards the close of the talk we often feel we haven't planned well enough, that the words are not clear in our mind, or that we are rushing because of time constraints. Consequently, our confidence dips at this critical stage. So, when we match this against what we know of the psychology of primacy and recency, we have a problem:

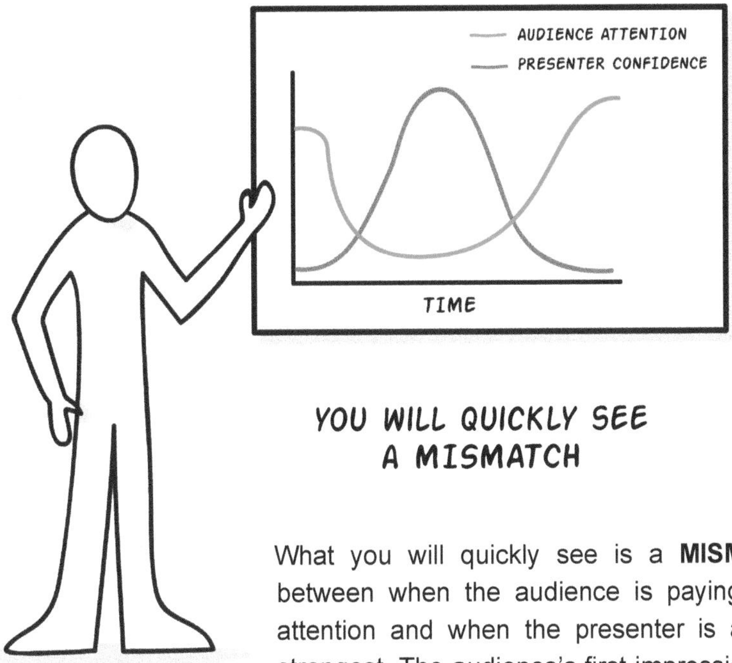

YOU WILL QUICKLY SEE A MISMATCH

What you will quickly see is a **MISMATCH** between when the audience is paying close attention and when the presenter is at their strongest. The audience's first impression is of a presenter looking a little uncertain and yet to find their flow. Likewise, as the audience becomes focused again towards the close, the presenter can often appear vague, hurried or lacking in confidence. For them, this is the most memorable part of the talk and this is the impression the audience will take away with them.

There is good news, however. The biggest challenge for any presenter or speaker is getting and keeping the audience's attention. In fact, the majority of the remainder of this book focuses on ways in which you can sustain the attention of your audience. But from our understanding of the primacy and recency effect, we know that for these two moments - the opening and the closing of your presentation - you will automatically have the audience's attention. Human psychology tells us that in these two moments you will be remembered without having to fight for attention.

The conclusion is obvious; as a presenter you must take time to craft and practice your opening and closing so that you take advantage of these two psychological principles. You need to open in a powerful, memorable and positive way. Then you need to give a very clear, very specific closing statement, preferably one that links to your opening.

1.5 Opening a presentation

Disappointingly, most people start with the classic opening by giving their name and introducing themselves with their job title or qualifications. This lacks impact and, if anything, tends to set a poor tone for the presentation. In their outstanding book ***Teach Yourself Presenting,*** Amanda Vickers and Steve Bavister write, *"just because most people do it, doesn't mean it's right, OR effective."*[16]

As mentioned earlier in the 'hints and tips' of section 1.3, one simple and effective way to make your opening much more impressive is simply to put the information that will grab the attention BEFORE your introduction. In other words, start immediately with your opening hook.

Your opening section should aim to achieve three things:

WAKE THEM UP

WIN THEM OVER

PREPARE THEM

Whilst it sounds easy, I know through personal experience that coming up with a creative and memorable opening can be hard work. Many people want to use humour to open their presentation but this needs to be done with great care and thought to ensure success! See chapter 3.6 on jokes and anecdotes for my recommendations. It is safer and more credible to use one of the following techniques to wake up your audience:

WAKE THEM UP

Ask them a question

This is a simple and straightforward way to get early engagement, but you must be sure about whether you expect an answer or whether the question is largely rhetorical.

"How many of you have woken up thinking about work?"

"What one word sums up your attitude towards health and safety?"

"If I could show you a way to earn more money, who here would be interested in hearing about it?" (Rhetorical)

SURPRISE or Shock

In general, unexpected statistics or facts are most effective for this category of opening. For maximum impact it is important that you do a little research to discover something that will truly surprise your audience.

"Just 23 customers account for 80% of our total income"

"Given current budgets, the total spend on technology last year would fund all staff training for the next 10 years!"

"Within 20 miles of where we are sitting there are 44 other companies offering a similar service to ours"

Intrigue

This is one of the trickier categories, but definitely a powerful technique when you have mastered it. Start by introducing a seemingly unconnected or unexpected subject, then transition smoothly and cleverly from your initial statement to the relevance it has to your topic.

"I'd like to speak with you about the importance of coffee"

"Today is one of the most terrifying days I have ever experienced, and when I tell you why you will most likely feel the same way"

"Our job is a lot like that of a dating agency"

Story

As we will see in chapter 5.4 storytelling is one of the most effective engagement techniques, and by far the simplest way to create a rapid connection with your audience. Make sure you select a story that won't take more than 2-3 minutes, and focus on moving from the story to its relevance to the topic you are presenting.

"Yesterday morning as I was driving, I passed a man with no car who was sitting on the side of the motorway on the hard shoulder..."

"I was sitting at my desk, deep in thought, when suddenly I heard a huge explosion. I jumped out of my seat, my heart pounding. As I ran out onto the shop floor I realised..."

"When I was a teenager my friends and I would always challenge each other to take bigger risks. I knew one day we'd get into real trouble, but I never realised how quickly things could change from fun to frightening..."

WIN THEM OVER

For this section we need to go back to our table in section 1.2 where we looked at the difference between what you care about and what the audience cares about. I introduced you to the acronym of WIIFM (what's in it for me). With this in mind, the first thing you need to do to 'win them over' is to make reference to what they are interested in and how your presentation will address these things. You need to explain, *in their terms* and from their perspective, why these things are important to them. Once you have clarified the importance of the subject to your audience, you may also need to emphasise the benefits to them. Many professionals assume that by explaining the importance, the benefits are automatically apparent. This isn't always the case. Explaining the benefits clearly will help motivate the audience to actively engage, rather than merely acknowledging that they *should* listen.

In addition to addressing the importance and the benefit of your presentation, you may need to justify your credentials - that is, who you are and why the audience should listen to you. You need to present yourself as someone credible and someone they should want to listen to/work with. Far too often speakers rely on seniority or qualifications to highlight their credibility. For many audiences this is either a) not as impactful as the speaker assumed or b) quite boring.

It is far better to consider these questions:

- **What qualifies you to be in front of this group?** ☐
- **What experiences have you had?** ☐
- **What successes and what failures?** ☐

These are much more relevant and, importantly, far more interesting to the audience.

For example:

"I have worked for this organisation for 10 years and before that I worked for two of our largest competitors. During my time with those other companies I saw some disasters. In fact, I was part of teams that made some huge mistakes. I learnt painful lessons the hard way, and over my 10 years with this business I've tried to keep those lessons at the front of my mind. I'd like to share with you what I've learnt and how you can avoid expensive, embarrassing mistakes!"

"Last year I joined this organisation hoping to use my engineering degree to impress my new employer. I quickly realised that there was a huge amount of experience within this organisation and the most important thing I could do was to become a great listener. So, I have spent the last 12 months listening to people like you. Today I'd like to hear your views and tell you about what I've heard from others."

Get creative and challenge yourself to answer the question, 'why should they listen to me?' Try to think of as many different options, then select the one(s) you believe will have the most impact on the audience.

Tell them why the subject is important to them

Tell them the benefits

State your credentials

'Winning them over' is less about you and much more about making sure the audience understand the importance of the subject!

PREPARE THEM

This is the final element of your opening and hopefully, the simplest. It is important to set the expectations for your audience. If this isn't done correctly there can be confusion and people can feel unsettled. By laying out a clear agenda you can pre-empt many questions. In addition, you can use the agenda as another opportunity to motivate and enthuse them about what is coming!

In terms of procedure, when to ask questions during your presentation is an important point. If you have a short time to present (for example less than 20 minutes) I strongly recommend making a clear request that the audience wait until the END to ask questions. Even just one or two questions along the way can put you under significant time pressure. In addition, very often the questions raised by the audience will actually be answered later on in your presentation. Under these circumstances, requesting that the audience hold their questions until the end can be very helpful. It is a good idea to ask the audience to write down any questions that come to mind as they think of them, so that they don't forget their question by the time you finish.

If your presentation is longer than 30 minutes, it is generally preferable to encourage the audience to ask questions WHILST you are speaking. This will make your presentation feel interactive and more like a conversation. This approach will have the effect of raising the engagement level of the audience and also give you real time feedback about their reaction to the talk. If you can think quickly while presenting, then the information provided by the questions can be hugely valuable in helping you frame and position the points you are about to go on to make.

- **Outline of topics or agenda**
- **Timings and/or duration of the session**
- **Procedure (when to ask questions, what notes or handouts are available etc.)**

In Summary:

You can use these techniques to take full advantage of the primacy effect, but you must not take too long in your delivery. With energy and a good pace **a great opening should take between 2 – 4 minutes**. You can accomplish a lot in this short time and when done well your audience will listen with enthusiasm, commitment and goodwill to what follows.

WAKE THEM UP

Ask them a question

Surprise or shock

Intrigue

Story

WIN THEM OVER

Tell them why the subject is important to them

Tell them the benefits

State your credentials

PREPARE THEM

Outline of topics or agenda

Timings and duration of the session

Procedure (asking questions, notes, handouts etc.)

1.6 Closing a presentation

Contrary to popular belief, putting up a slide with 'QUESTIONS?' does not constitute a powerful close to your presentation. We've considered how to take advantage of the primacy effect and now we'll consider the recency effect. Research has shown the recency effect is stronger than the primacy effect because it takes advantage of short term memory. So, you need to think very carefully about your closing words and requests because these are what will stick with your audience. They will remember not only what you said, but also the impression you gave as you said it.

More and more presenters are grasping the idea of the 'big close'. Unfortunately, they generally incorporate only 50% of the important elements that a great close needs. The mistake I see time and time again is a close which is ultimately all style and no substance. This trend seems to have developed from the world of motivational speaking and has moved into political speaking: the speaker builds up the energy, fires up the crowd and at the crescendo delivers a seemingly powerful but largely empty request or statement. These closings often run along the lines of, "go out and believe in yourself", "so let's go and make a real difference to this company", "together we can achieve great things", and so on. The sentiment is admirable, and certainly for a short time afterwards the audience feels 'the buzz', but soon normal life resumes and those sentiments are of little practical use.

A great close certainly *can* be delivered with a big impact, but it can be equally powerful when spoken very quietly from the heart. The key is in the substance of the message. You must ensure you are both **clear** and **specific** about what you expect from your audience.

A great closing will do these things:

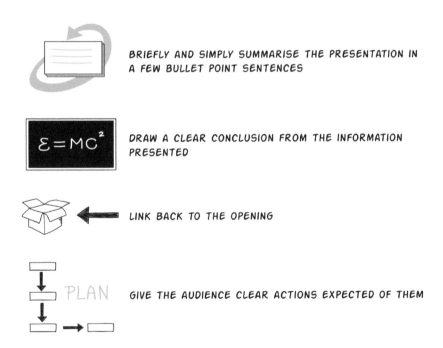

BRIEFLY AND SIMPLY SUMMARISE THE PRESENTATION IN A FEW BULLET POINT SENTENCES

DRAW A CLEAR CONCLUSION FROM THE INFORMATION PRESENTED

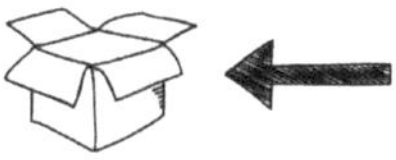

LINK BACK TO THE OPENING

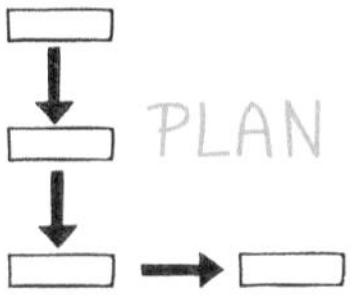

GIVE THE AUDIENCE CLEAR ACTIONS EXPECTED OF THEM

Even with this simple description, I've found presenters can be unclear with their action request. Take, for example, "I want you to go out and think about the ways you can really live the values of this company." Phrases like 'think about' are simply too vague for an audience to respond to, and are unlikely to create any meaningful change. Compare it to a more specific request: "Next time you meet a new colleague, take a few minutes to introduce yourself and find out a little about that person. This will really show others that you are living the values of the company." Now the audience has a clear idea of what is expected of them. Even if meeting a new colleague isn't relevant to every person in that audience, because the example is specific and contextualised it makes the idea more concrete in their minds.

A final point to consider: as we will see in chapter 6, many presenters will have a question and answer session at the end of their presentation. Always ensure that *before* you finish you **repeat your closing**, word for word if necessary, at the end of the questions section. Remember the nature of the recency effect; the last few pieces of information will stick in the audience's short term memory, but the final question and answer is unlikely to be the important message you want people to remember!

1.7 The role of technology and slides

As mentioned in section 1.3, technology such as slides are best used to:

- Simplify and summarise the content for the audience
- Visualise your ideas

These are the two strongest reasons why a presenter would consider using slides or visual technologies. Anything that serves the purpose of visualising content or summarising key points is likely to be useful (assuming you keep the total number of slides to an absolute minimum!).

There are two additional reasons why presenters use technology:

- To give structure and direction
- Because it's expected

Whilst both are somewhat valid as additional reasons to use slides, I also have reservations which I'll explain.

Structure and direction

Many speakers appreciate the reassurance slides give them. If they forget their words or what is coming next, then the slides can cue them. Having these prompts visible on a screen can be helpful. It is also quite simple and convenient to reorder slides to create a more effective narrative, altering the flow of the presentation. Whilst this can be beneficial, I believe the negatives far outweigh the positives when using slides to help with structure and direction.

During your presentation you are constantly receiving feedback from your audience; either verbally through questions or non-verbally through body language. In response to this feedback, a great speaker will adapt their delivery to focus on the areas which are of most interest to the audience. For example, a lot of questions about a particular topic might encourage you to spend a little longer on that subject. Or if, during a particular section of your presentation, people start checking their phones and looking bored you will quickly move on to your next point.

When an audience is engaged with your presentation the discussion can go in many different directions. Unfortunately, the same can't be said for the software. Unless you have an advanced level of technical knowledge slides can only go in two directions - forwards or backwards. I regularly see presenters so wedded to their slides that they plough on through their delivery regardless of the signals from the audience. By creating the slide deck, the presentation is fixed in their brain and they feel they must deliver that presentation exactly as planned. This rigidity disconnects them from the audience and prevents them noticing any feedback. On more than one occasion I have seen a presenter come to a slide, look surprised, and then say something along the lines of "this slide isn't really relevant to you, but what it's showing is ... (followed by explanation)." Even though the slide isn't relevant they cover the content anyway because it is there. This is simply crazy.

Great speakers are aware of the signals and feedback from the audience and, in response, they have the courage to switch off the slides if they are not relevant or if the conversation takes a different direction. When speakers use slides as a form of 'autocue' they lose the flexibility to respond to their audience and their presentation becomes a one-way lecture. This is not to say that you must always be led by your audience. There will be times when the audience needs to understand the content even though they find it boring, and other times when your audience tries to direct the discussion off-topic and away from your agenda. For those occasions you should use the techniques discussed in chapter 3 on audience engagement.

It's expected

When I challenge people about WHY they are using slides, the prevailing response is "my boss/company requires slides so there is a record of my presentation". This is essentially a kind of paper trail to ensure there is a record of what was said and that notes that can be circulated. If you have been told by your organisation or boss that you must have slides, I'd encourage you to challenge that request and find out if it is a preference or an absolute requirement. Could you, for example, provide handouts instead of slides? Usually you will find that there isn't an actual rule stating that all presentation have slides. If there is a rule it is rare for the mandate to be limited to slides only; most companies will be happy with any hard copy summary of your presentation.

Why am I making a big deal about this? Slides have become a ubiquitous feature of our organisational presentations and audiences have become numb to them. This potential cost is huge. Henley Management College calculated that, in the UK alone, if the average manager spends one hour a week talking to an inattentive audience in a meeting then the total cost to British industry is £7.8bn a year. Professional speaking coach Max Atkinson firmly points the finger of blame at slide shows: "In a lot of organisations it's not regarded as a proper presentation unless there's slides". In the same BBC News article audiences are described as having "glazed expressions elicited by an army of PowerPoint-crazed middle managers".

I understand that there are cultural norms in our organisations but I also believe that by abandoning slides and technology you have a fantastic opportunity to stand out from your peer group and wake up your audiences. As we will discuss in chapter 6, there are many other techniques you can use to dramatise and support your delivery.

In summary, only when you have fully prepared the content of your presentation as outlined in chapter 1.3 should you consider which points could benefit from a visual. Chapter 7 is dedicated to this subject, and chapter 2.6 addresses how to present effectively alongside the technology.

1.8 The effect of room layout

The layout of the room is incredibly important, but it is consistently overlooked by presenters. I've been running seminars on this subject for many years, and I'm astounded by how few people have actually considered the impact and logic behind room layout.

There are two reasons why this is so critical. Firstly, the room layout you select will have a direct impact on the behaviour and energy level of the audience. You need to consider your desired outcome and design your layout accordingly. Secondly, if you don't have control over the room layout, it is essential that you understand how the layout will encourage certain behaviours. By understanding how different layouts work you can prepare for this and compensate by adapting your style or methodology.

The following sections cover the most common room layout options and the impact they have on a group.

U-shape or Horseshoe

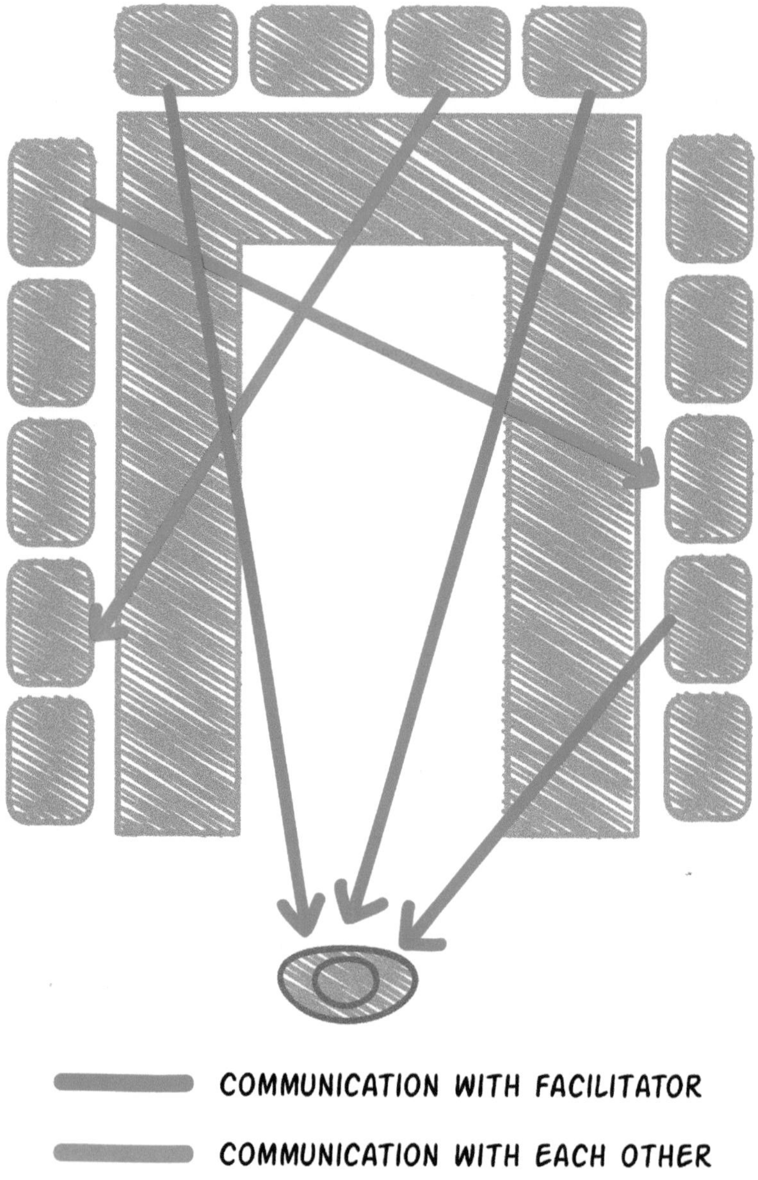

Best suited to:

- Training courses
- Technical updates and briefings
- Facilitator led sessions

Advantages

The u-shape has two major advantages:

1. Everyone can see everyone else. Eye contact can be made with virtually everyone in the group, creating a sense of equality.
2. The presenter can easily keep control of the audience because they are the focus.

Disadvantages

- Because everyone can see everyone else, anything said by an audience member is very 'public'. Unless there is an exceptionally high level of trust it can be very hard to get an open conversation started. Even asking questions to the group might be initially met with silence.
- This layout takes up a large amount of space. A big room is needed to ensure there is adequate space between the chairs and the walls.
- Groupwork is difficult. Inevitably, groups can only be formed by working along each side of the 'u' shape and teams are limited to 3 or 4 people to ensure they can all see and hear each other. If you are in this situation it's a good idea to place a few chairs on the inside of the 'u', then you can ask some audience members to sit there during group work.

Cabaret style or Table groups

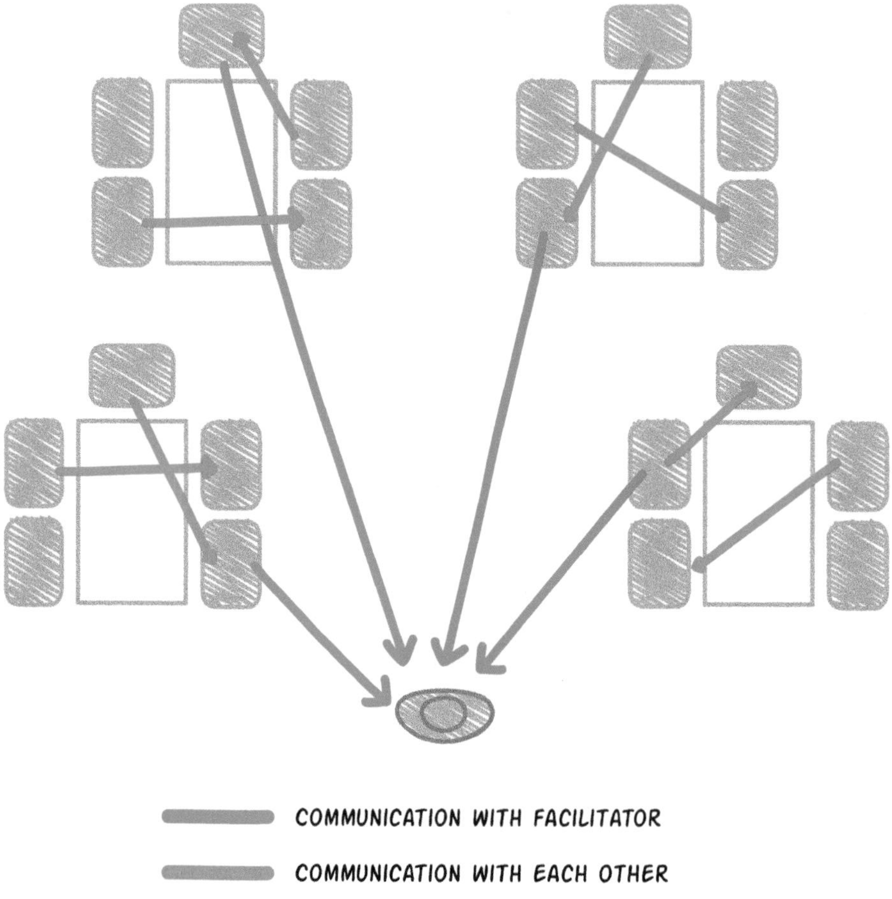

Best suited to:

- Team events and team building
- Sensitive subjects where you want audience members to give you honest, truthful feelings
- Cynical, quiet or low energy audiences

Advantages

Working in this style has two major advantages:

1. People will start talking from the instant they sit down, so it's great for groupwork and high energy work.

1. Groups can speak very honestly to each other because it's more 'private'. Any feedback given to the facilitator is on behalf of the group and therefore safer.

Disadvantages

- Difficult for the facilitator to maintain eye contact with the whole audience and for the audience members to see each other.
- Higher energy within groups means it is harder for the facilitator to keep control - expect side conversations and interruptions.
- The tabled groups quickly become 'teams' and can begin to exclude those on other tables. To avoid this it is essential to mix the groups up more than once throughout the session to avoid 'cliques' developing.

Theatre or Classroom style

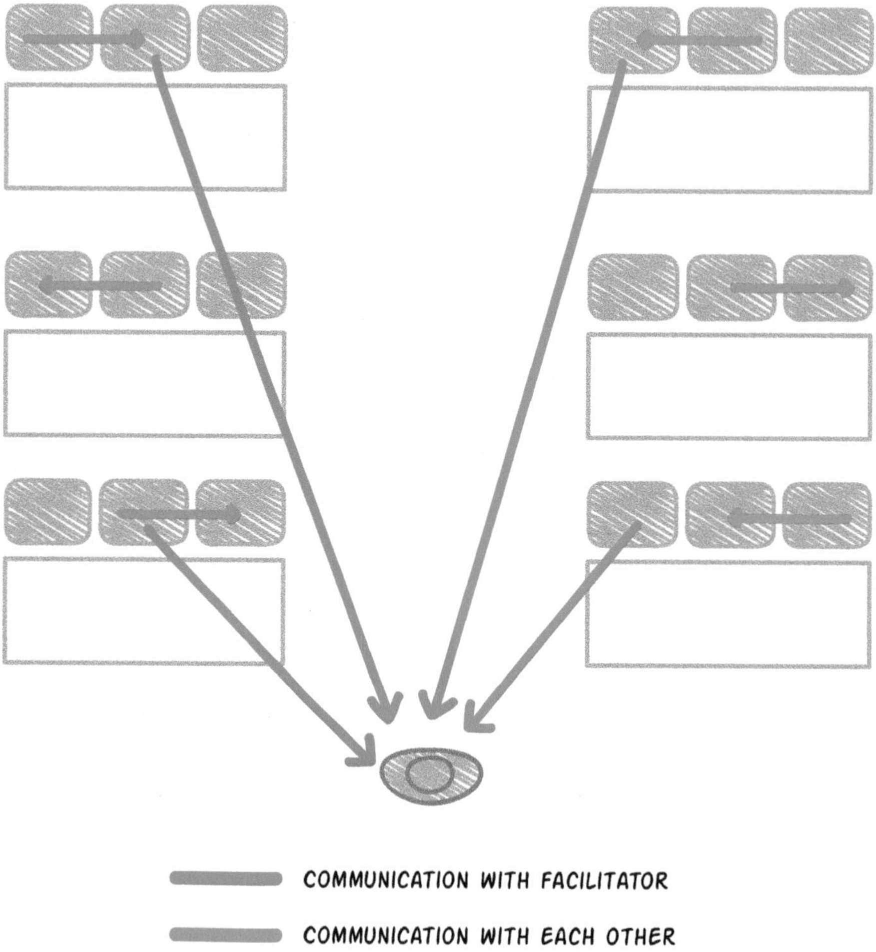

Best suited to:

- One way corporate updates and 'town hall' style communications
- Unruly audiences who might be at risk of side tracking or disrupting the intended agenda
- Smaller spaces

Advantages

The theatre setup has two major advantages:

1. It makes efficient use of space and can therefore accommodate more people than the other styles.
2. It maintains a high level of control over the audience and reduces the likelihood of conversation.

Disadvantages

- Audience members will likely fall into a classroom mindset and will sit quietly listening. Don't expect them to engage in lively conversation!
- It is very difficult for the audience members to see each other; most will be looking at the back of heads.
- Groupworking becomes limited to working with the people sitting either side. A useful tip: if you find yourself in this situation, create groups of four by asking two people in front to turn around to work with the two people sitting behind them.

CHAPTER SUMMARY

PURPOSE

Be clear about the purpose of your presentation, both from the organisational and audience perspective. What is the result that you are aiming to achieve?

AUDIENCE

Be aware of the audience profile, their attitude, knowledge and expectations. If necessary, do some brief research phone calls in advance to get a feel for the people you will be presenting to.

STRUCTURE

Structure your presentations using the OMEC Model as a framework: Open – Message – Evidence – Close. For longer presentations you can have up to three cycles of 'message – evidence' covering three key points before continuing to your close.

PRIMACY/RECENCY

The primacy and recency effect emphasises how important it is that you prepare, develop and practise your opening and closing. During these periods of time the audience's attention is 'gifted' to you by our psychology, it is important to grab them – you don't have time to warm up and find your stride!

For references and links from this chapter visit chris-atkinson.co.uk/books

OPENINGS

Openings are primarily about grabbing attention. If you put the attention - grabbing ahead of your personal introduction and agenda you will be more creative and interesting.

CLOSINGS

Your closing must focus on the specific call to action, what specifically is it that you would like the audience to do (behaviour) as a result of your presentation? To look really professional link your closing to your opening theme/message.

TECHNOLOGY

Remember that the role of slides and technology is to *support* you by providing visuals and highlighting key points. Don't allow the technology to lead your presentation, create your presentation first then ask "what visuals do I need to support my delivery?"

ROOM LAYOUT

The room layout will significantly alter the way the audience behaves in the session. If you have the ability to adapt the room, then choose the layout that will work best for the style of your presentation. If you can't change the layout of the room, then consider carefully the likely impact of the layout you have been given and how you can make the best of it!

1

CHAPTER

2

PRESENTING WITH IMPACT

Before we can start looking at the techniques we can use to engage and inspire, we need a strong foundation in presentation basics. The skills covered in this chapter may in fact be the hardest to master. They will take great patience, a lot of practice, and a positive attitude! These skills will ensure that you are, first and foremost, calm and in control. They will also ensure that you look professional and are essential in communicating the enthusiasm you want to show.

2.1 Vital statistics and half-truths

When we communicate, what percentage of that communication is achieved through the words we choose? How much is in our body language? And what about our voice? You may now be trying to recall these statistics from a training course sometime in your past. Perhaps a vague recollection that 'words' are not as important as we often think.

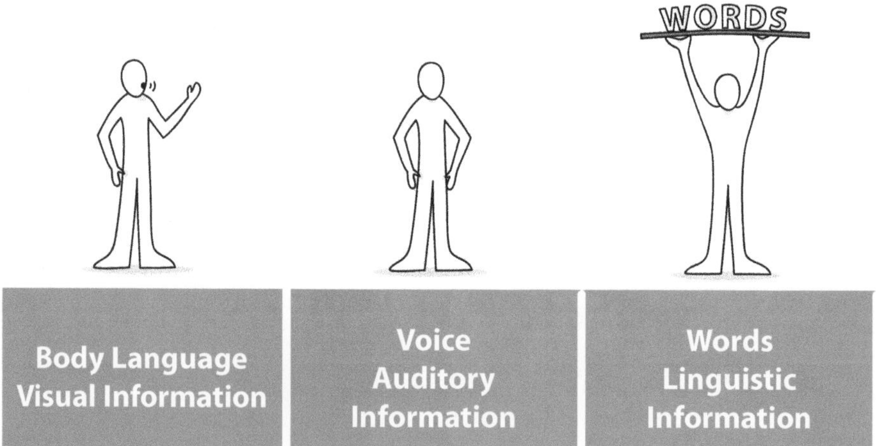

Well, the famous study you are trying to recall is known as the Mehrabian study, based on the work of Dr Albert Mehrabian at UCLA[18]. A statistic from his work caught the attention of the public and became a consistent and predictable part of training programmes worldwide.

Our words account for only 7% of our communication

That certainly *should* be very headline grabbing

...if it were true!

In fact, the second most famous thing about this study is that it is consistently misquoted and misrepresented. A quick internet search on "the Mehrabian Myth" will reveal the controversy and debate which quickly followed the mass popularisation and subsequent misrepresentation of the study.

Mehrabian's experiment was not intended to be a blanket statement about **all** communication; it was conducted in a very specific way and tested only a very specific set of circumstances. I'd hope you would agree that a large part of the *meaning* of communication must lie within the message itself. The question that should in fact interest us, and the one that interested Mehrabian is: *What happens when those communication channels of voice, body, and words are not in agreement?* In other words, what happens when we say one thing but our voice and body language communicate something different?

The answer to this question is much more interesting, and one we'll discuss further in a moment. The important points can easily get lost within the debate about the validity of the study itself. We don't want to get too hung up on the literal percentages in Mehrabian's results. What we need to understand is that differing circumstances affect the relationship between words, voice and body language messages.

In his fascinating psychology book ***The Man Who Mistook his Wife for a Hat***, Oliver Sacks[19] recounts observing a group of patients suffering from brain damage, who were watching the President of the United States speak on television and roaring with laughter. One group of these people were aphasics; they had largely lost the ability to understand language. They could, however, still effectively process the voice tone or visual cues of communication. *"Their friends, their relatives, the nurses who knew them well, could hardly believe, sometimes, that they were aphasic. This was because, when addressed naturally, they grasped some or most of the meaning. And one does speak 'naturally', naturally."*

So what was the cause of their laughter? Why the reaction?

To these people there was no congruence between the tones and gestures. It was so false that it appeared to them as total nonsense.

As Sacks puts it: "*In this, then, lies their power of understanding — understanding, without words, what is authentic or inauthentic. Thus it was the grimaces, the false gestures and, above all, the false tones and cadences of the voice, which rang false for these wordless but immensely sensitive patients. It was to these (for them) most glaring, even grotesque, incongruities and improprieties that my aphasic patients responded, undeceived and undeceivable by words.*"

But there was another group of people on the ward who were perplexed by the speech in a different way. This group of people had lost the ability to understand tone and inflexion in communication. They only understood the pure language, with none of the subtlety of the emotional tone of that communication. One such patient was Emily D. She also had much to say about the President: "*Emily D. also listened, stony-faced, to the President's speech, bringing to it a strange mixture of enhanced and defective perceptions — precisely the opposite mixture to those of our aphasiacs. It did not move her — no speech now moved her — and all that was evocative, genuine or false completely passed her by. Deprived of emotional reaction, was she then (like the rest of us) transported or taken in? By no means. 'He is not cogent,' she said. 'He does not speak good prose. His word-use is improper. Either he is brain-damaged, or he has something to conceal.' Thus the President's speech did not work for Emily D. either, due to her enhanced sense of formal language use, propriety as prose, any more than it worked for our aphasiacs, with their word-deafness but enhanced sense of tone.*"

So whatever the statistics and whatever your personal beliefs, it is ESSENTIAL that you demonstrate congruence and authenticity in the marriage of your words, voice and body language. All three channels need to be broadcasting the same message.

Moreover, as you will see in the following pages it is likely you will need to present in a 'bigger' way than feels comfortable. Many people are shocked by how different the reaction of an audience is when they simply increase body language, voice and emphasis in their presentation style. Researchers Kouzes and Posner[20] studied charisma over many years, and conclude "*People who are perceived to be charismatic are simply more animated than others. They smile more, speak faster, pronounce words more clearly, and move their heads and bodies more often.*"

So be animated in verbal delivery and gestures, put a smile on your face, have energy in your step and enthusiasm about your subject.

2.2 Handling nerves and anxiety

> “ *The terror of performing never goes away. Instead, you get very, very comfortable being terrified.* **Eric Whitacre**

I want to be honest now and give you some potentially bad news - if you are looking for a cure for butterflies and nervousness, I don't have it. Moreover, I'm not sure I want it. I've been a professional speaker all of my working life, I deliver hundreds of presentations each year and I always feel a certain level of anxiety about speaking. I don't regard this as a bad thing however, because that anxiety reminds me that the audience has expectations and that I can't take their attention or interest for granted. I have to work for it!

In 2014 the Hollywood film director Michael Bay took to the stage for an interview at the Consumer Electronics Show in Las Vegas, the world's largest gadget expo. Since his first movie (Bad Boys in 1995) he has become one of the best known action movie directors. Bay commands some of the largest budgets of any movies produced worldwide including the Transformers movies, Pearl Harbour and Armageddon. Unfortunately for Michael, as he walked onstage there was a momentary confusion about who would speak first (Michael or the interviewer) and, as a result, the autocue machine failed. For any speaker this would create a moment of hesitation but luckily the quick thinking interviewer (Joe Stinziano, Samsung's executive vice president) stepped in and asked Michael a simple question:

"You're known for such unbelievable action, what inspires you? How do you come up with these unbelievable ideas?"

How challenging do you think that is to answer for a man at the top of his profession who, for over 20 years, has been passionate about big screen storytelling? Well, what actually happened was an entirely human response; in front of hundreds of journalists and industry professionals Bay froze. With no autocue he stumbled over his words, became acutely stressed and walked off stage. In total it was a little over one minute from walking on stage to leaving. You will find many articles about this incident online as well as video footage. It prompted much debate about the stress and fear associated with presenting.

Now, use your imagination for a moment to picture this scene: Michael Bay is at a dinner party with a mixed group of professionals and movie industry types.

During the chat over the meal another diner leans over and asks him that exact question; “What inspires you and how do you come up with these unbelievable ideas?” Do you think he would panic, stumble and leave the table? Of course not, I am 100% certain he would answer the question fully, passionately and in a calm natural way. Why is that? What is so different about the onstage experience that seems to ‘short circuit’ our ability to think and speak as we would in any normal circumstance? Well, there is a deep biological influence at play when we stand in front of groups and have all eyes on us, it provokes a core evolutionary response that is extremely powerful and can be very damaging in our modern day environment.

We can imagine stress as a ‘n-shaped’ curve:

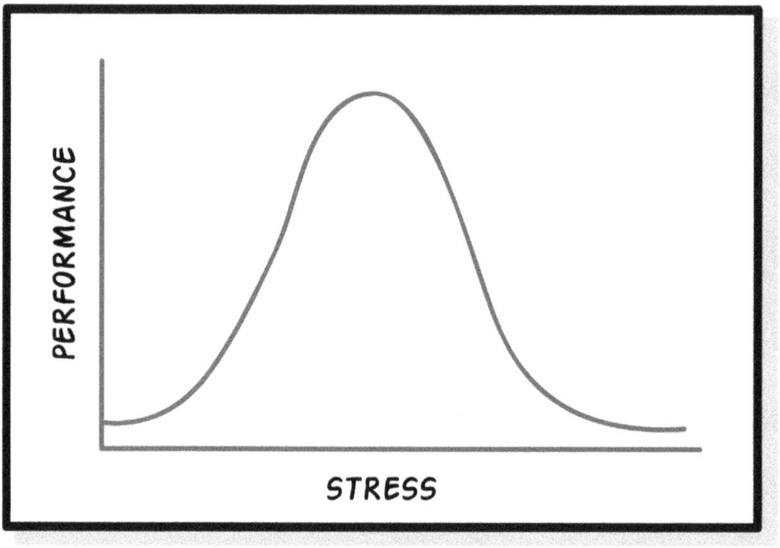

If we don’t feel any stress we could become overconfident, complacent and not prepare properly. We may deliver our presentation in a lazy way or perhaps appear arrogant by failing to connect with the audience. In contrast, a little stress can actually help our performance by making us more alert, more aware of our circumstances and our audience. Unfortunately, at the far end of the curve we know that too much stress and anxiety can overwhelm people, causing them to freeze, forget their content or feel physically sick.

The skill that all the best speakers, facilitators and leaders have is the ability to conceal from the audience their internal anxieties. Unless you show it on the outside, the audience won’t know how you feel. The only way for the audience to know that you are nervous or anxious is through your body language, your voice or if you tell them in your words.

Over the years you've probably been told about the importance of a positive mental attitude. The received wisdom is that you need to get into a strong frame of mind by using visualisation techniques, positive mantras, pep talks and so on. Although I know these do work for some people, I've not found them very useful for my own psychology; trying to tell my brain to feel confident was never very effective. In fact, I became fascinated by the reverse approach: how your body behaviour has an impact on your attitude. The technique we are about to discuss doesn't put you in conflict with your natural feelings. Quite simply, if you adopt the traits of a confident person your mind actually starts to feel more confident. In other words, our behaviour impacts our attitude.[21]

In her Harvard Business School article ***Power Posing: Brief Nonverbal Displays Affect Neuroendocrine Levels and Risk Tolerance,***[22] HBS assistant professor Amy J C Cuddy demonstrates this principle. She found that simply holding your body in expansive, "high-power" poses stimulates higher levels of testosterone (the hormone linked to power and dominance in the animal and human worlds) and lower levels of cortisol (the "stress" hormone). The result? In addition to causing the desired hormonal shift, the power poses led to increased feelings of power. The conclusion of the article supports my message: *"People tend to spend too much energy focusing on the words they're saying — perfectly crafting the content of the message — when in many cases that matters much less than how it's being communicated. People often are more influenced by how they feel about you than by what you're saying. It's not about the content of the message, but how you're communicating it."*

Self-awareness and self-management are the key components here. The symptoms of anxiety are exhibited differently for different people. Here are some I've come across:

- Talking too fast
- Talking in a monotone voice
- Talking too quietly
- Increasing pulse rate
- Fast breathing
- Dry mouth

- Feeling sick
- Sweaty palms
- Needing the toilet
- Loss of vocabulary
- Shaking
- Flushing of face or chest

The list goes on in many more weird and wonderful ways depending on who you talk to! It is important you know what your stress responses are, and that you learn to be comfortable with them as well as manage them. I understand that when you find yourself in front of a 'live' audience it is not a very convenient time to explore these issues and to experiment, so I strongly recommend you find offline opportunities to get comfortable with the inevitable feelings of self-consciousness. By 'offline opportunities' I refer to times when you might experience the same anxious feelings but where there are little or no negative career consequences! At the more daring end of the spectrum you might consider:

- Theatre groups
- Stand-up comedy or improvisation groups
- Open mic nights
- Choirs
- Business networking groups
- Professional speaking associations

Although some of these may seem a bit unusual, you will be surprised how many local groups there are doing exactly these things within 30 minutes of your home. As a simple example, reading a printed poem at an open mic/ poetry night gives you an opportunity to experience and manage your anxiety without the worry about content or professional credibility.

My favourite recommendation is much more accessible than these suggestions, and arguably more powerful, because you are in complete control of the experience.

Stand at the front of a theatre or cinema before the show begins.

That's it! Just go to the front, preferably the centre (but you can work up to that) and stand there facing the crowd for as long as you can bear it. While you are there look at the audience, take it all in slowly, become aware of the feelings, become aware of your body and start to practice the body language techniques covered in the next chapter. This is a fantastic technique and so easy to do - if you do it in the cinema it's even dark! The key thing to remember here is that ***no one cares about you*** (sorry); you are simply somebody standing at the front, probably looking for a friend, or maybe a weirdo, but nobody relevant to them. If anxiety affects you, go and do this - and keep doing it. Eventually the sensations will change for you.

Much of our experience of nervousness and this tendency to feel anxious about standing in front of a group can be accounted for by a psychological phenomenon known as "the spotlight effect". The spotlight effect describes our tendency to forget that although we are the centre of our own world, we are not the centre of everyone else's. As a result, we significantly over-estimate the amount of attention and importance that other people give to us. For a simple example, think of a time when you had a spot or pimple prominently visible on your face. When you walked past people you felt self-conscious, perhaps you were certain they would notice it, you may have even gone out of your way to hide it or avoided meeting people. This is the spotlight effect in action; other people are significantly less interested in your face than you are!

When you are feeling anxious you are mostly thinking about yourself and often this feeling will be accompanied by a physical adrenaline reaction. All of your attention becomes focused on your internal world or dialogue and the adrenaline makes it hard to shift your attention elsewhere. For example, you might start to think about:

- How do I look?
- What are the audience thinking of me?
- What am I going to say next?

As you get locked into this cycle of thought you will become more and more anxious. You are also forgetting the single most important fact about presenting: **It's not about you, it's about the audience!**

In summary, your focus on yourself is drawing your attention to entirely the wrong area. The audience really isn't that interested in you as such, they have their own selfish thoughts of "what's in it for me?". Your number one priority is to consider: What do the audience need? How are they responding? The huge benefit of this is that human attention is a limited resource and, in general, can only be applied in one direction. By focusing your attention on your audience you are shifting attention away from yourself and therefore you will quickly feel less anxious. In addition, the added sensitivity to the needs of your audience will make you a much better presenter!

2.3 What to do with your hands and feet

So here's a strange thing: how often in 'normal life' (chatting to friends, going out, working etc.) do you become self-conscious or uncomfortable about what to do with your hands and feet? I'm guessing the answer is hardly ever! One of the marvellous things about our biology is our brain's ability to take care of these things without our conscious awareness.

Unfortunately, that all changes when we stand up in front of people. Sadly, under these circumstances, our conscious brain performs staggeringly worse than our unconscious brain. Most people immediately become 'self' conscious; we become far more aware of our body and how it looks. As a result, quite suddenly, our hands and legs can become quite awkward, we shuffle around on our feet, adopt unusual poses and hold our hands in various positions in an attempt to alleviate our discomfort.

Keeping the previous chapters in mind, we know that it is critical that your body language and words are in agreement, so let's address this issue. The good news is that it is a straightforward fix. There is an overwhelming preference by audiences about how they want speakers to stand and speak. You will see this posture in most good presentation technique and body language books. Quite simply, you should stand with your feet about a shoulder width apart, with your hips central, your hands to your sides and your head looking forward towards your audience, as shown.

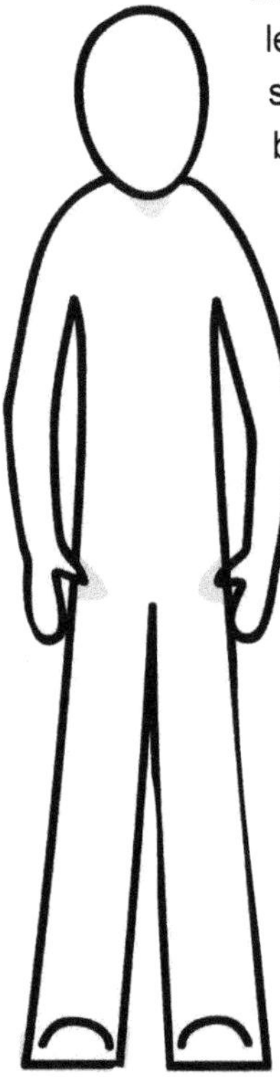

From this point on I will refer to this posture as 'the parking position' because it is rather like parking a car. When you are not driving, you put the gear stick in neutral. This posture is your 'neutral', so when you are not using a part of your body to present you 'park it' in this position.

Reassuringly, textbooks and professionals are all in agreement on this posture.[23]

I have found, however, that all major books on the subject miss out one critical piece of information.

PARKING POSITION

This simple omission has negatively affected the millions of people worldwide who have been given this (correct) advice on effective body language. The missing information is this:

It will *FEEL* wrong!!

Give it a go right now. Stand in exactly the posture illustrated, with your feet flat on the floor, your hands by your sides and your eyes looking straight ahead. Don't move or fidget. Hold it for as long as feels comfortable.

How natural did it feel? How long did your arms feel?

The problem with this posture is that whilst this genuinely looks the strongest and most professional to the audience, it feels wrong to the presenter. As a result, presenters often assume is must also look wrong. In fact, the assumption that things that look good will also feel good (and vice versa) is problematic. This is why all good presentation skills training courses will use video cameras; they provide visual evidence proving that the posture which felt uncomfortable to you looks strong and confident to the viewer.

So what's going on with our psychology here? It's quite straightforward really: it's unlikely that you will have spent much time standing in this posture before, so it feels unnatural. All you need to do is practice this parking position and the other body language recommendations in this chapter until they start to feel more natural and more comfortable.

In chapter 2.2 we discussed how adopting a strong, confident body language will actually start to make you feel stronger and more confident. The parking position sends a powerful message to your subconscious and by maintaining that posture you avoid 'leakage' in your body language i.e. behaviours that give away what you are really feeling. Here are some examples of typical leakage in body language:

- Shuffling feet
- Shifting weight from leg to leg
- Rubbing hands
- Playing with hair or jewellery
- Playing with things in pockets
- Not holding eye contact

Most common examples of less effective postures:

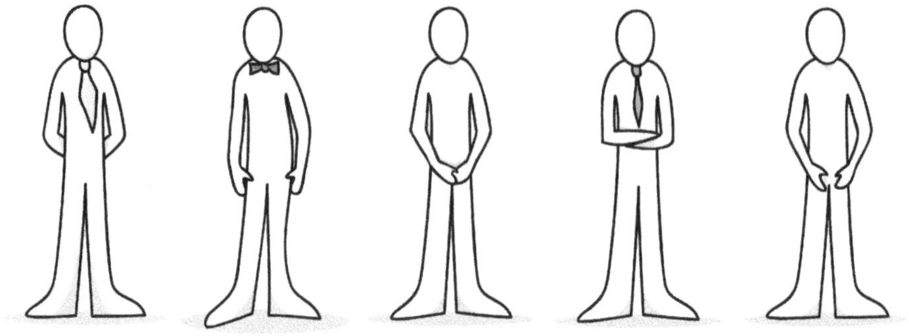

LESS EFFECTIVE POSITIONS

Speakers also get remarkably self-conscious about arm movements. Along with facial expressions, arms and hands are hugely expressive in communication. Our gestures are constantly communicating to the audience - sometimes deliberately, sometimes unconsciously! Very often speakers say one thing with their words but use gestures that do not reflect the same meaning. This creates incongruence and, as we saw in chapter 2.1, congruence is critical for influencing and engaging an audience.

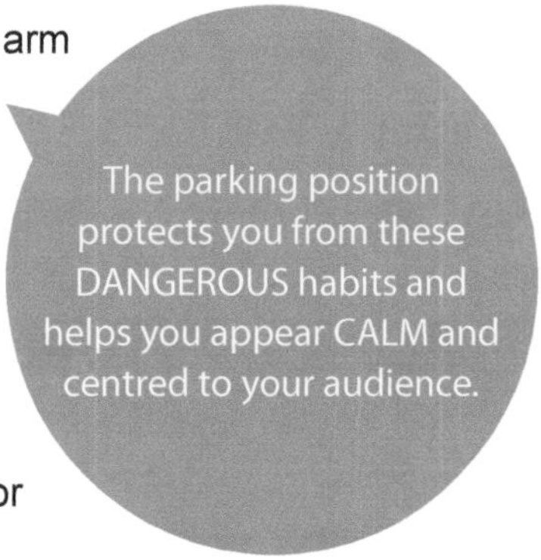
The parking position protects you from these DANGEROUS habits and helps you appear CALM and centred to your audience.

For example, if you say "large increase", your gestures need to be *large*! If you say "increase", your gestures should match by going *up* or *expanding*. In this way, almost any words can have congruent movements associated; reduce, parallel, in the past, in the future, today and so on. As an exercise, imagine you had to communicate with no words, using only gestures. How would you get your message across? You need to point your gestures in the right direction (although let's not move towards 'charades' just yet!).

People I work with often assume that if they use large hand gestures they will look like an over-the-top evangelist speaker. This simply isn't true; what feels like a huge gesture to you will look powerful and strong to the audience. A simple principle for good hand and arm use is to try to open your elbows as often as possible. Too many speakers have 'sticky elbows' where their elbows remain fixed to the sides of their body like a T-Rex. Ensuring your elbows are away from your body and that your arms are extended will demonstrate your confidence. Use slower, deliberate movements; fast, jerky movements will look nervous.

Should I Move Around?

I often find speakers who say they prefer walking around when they speak - in other words, they feel calmer and more comfortable pacing the floor. These speakers will go to great lengths to persuade themselves that the audience also prefers this because it makes them look more relaxed and more interesting. NO!!! Unless you are on a large stage with a huge audience you should never pace around like a caged lion, it drives audiences crazy! Moreover, it makes you look uncomfortable. I understand that it makes *you* feel more comfortable, but it most certainly does not have that effect on your audience. Learn to stand still and control unnecessary movements in any part of your body.

There is a simple rule for movement: ***Make sure it has purpose!***

This doesn't mean you have to be a statue in front of the audience - far from it. Your body is a great communication tool and when speaking your upper body and face should be animated and full of life. There is very little you can do with legs and feet that will enhance your communication so if you don't have a reason for moving, don't move.

2.4 The power of eye contact and pausing

Eye contact

For many people, eye contact can be an uncomfortable part of speaking. Over the years there has been a lot of bad advice given, which appears to have stayed in the public consciousness.

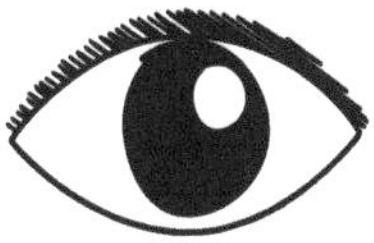

These bad techniques include:

- Scanning the audience, sweeping eye contact across the room
- Looking slightly above each person's head
- Looking at the wall behind each person
- Looking to the back of the room

All of these spell disaster for modern speakers because they are all techniques to manage anxiety and nerves. They are absolutely not focused on the one thing a speaker should really care about - *connecting with your audience*. Too many speakers avoid eye contact; many favour looking at the floor or ceiling. So if you find yourself noting the light fixtures or admiring the pattern on the carpet, you are probably missing the eye contact opportunity!

Eye contact is potentially the most important emotional connection you can have with your audience. You do not want to let nervousness and anxiety get in the way of that opportunity. Speakers are generally nervous about eye contact because they are worried about what they might see - boredom, disagreement, anger and so on. In my experience, the opposite is true. Whenever I work with a speaker to help them use eye contact effectively, the audience responds by paying more attention to them and some nod or smile encouragingly. It is actually a wonderful way to *increase* your confidence.

The most effective use of eye contact is simply to speak to each audience member for a few seconds (try counting to 3) then moving on to someone else. Avoid working your way around the group in any recognisable pattern e.g. left to right or front to back. Rather, pick different people at random and talk to that person until you recognise a connection. Each individual will feel it and, more amazingly, so will the entire group.

What about really large groups?

Let's imagine you have a group of 50-100 people. It isn't possible to make eye contact with each person individually. So what do you do? Well actually, you don't do anything differently! Even with groups of more than 200 people, I simply make sure I'm connecting with as many individuals as possible. I still maintain eye contact until I believe they've acknowledged the connection (2-3 seconds normally) then I move on to someone else. With larger groups, audience members can feel anonymous and can be easily distracted by things such as phones. Using direct eye contact can bring these people back into the presentation. More importantly, the people sitting around them will also feel the connection you are making and will be drawn into the presentation.

Pausing

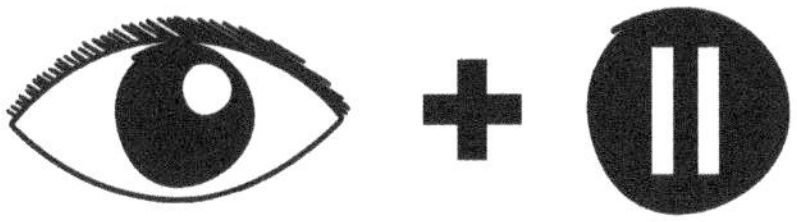

When combined with good eye contact, effective use of **pausing** can significantly increase the impact of your presentation and raise your level of professionalism. Much like eye contact, a good pause should last for a slow count to three before continuing. Pausing is essential for a number of reasons. Firstly, many speakers start using 'umm' and 'err' when they're nervous to fill in the gaps between words. We use these noises whilst we're searching for the correct word or phrase and they help us to feel more comfortable about the gaps in our speech. Unfortunately these filler noises make us appear nervous and unsure. The solution to 'umming' and 'erring' is to learn to pause and be silent whilst you are forming your next sentence. It is astounding how a nervous speaker can be transformed into a powerful presence just by replacing umms with quiet pauses.

When you pause the audience thinks and reflects on what you have just said. So, logically, if you never pause in a presentation the audience will never have the opportunity to think about your content. The audience will be carried along until you stop and then they will recall very little. A strategic pause after a particular message emphasises the importance of that message, and indicates to the audience that they are expected to think about what you have just said.

Another reason why we absolutely MUST pause and which is often missed:

Question:

What is the audience doing whilst you are pausing?

Answer:

...Thinking

?

A final reason to pause is to give yourself time to think! Speaking without pausing is, for many people, like accelerating out of control down a hill. The faster you speak the faster you have to think. The less time you have to think the less happy you will be about what you are saying, and the more stressed and anxious you will feel. Give yourself time! Pause, look at the audience (not at the floor or ceiling) and collect your thoughts, and then continue speaking. The audience will assume you did it for impact and weight and you will look amazing!

2.5 Using your voice to best effect

Your voice is an incredible instrument and one that receives surprisingly little attention when you consider how much of everyday life involves verbal communication. It is essential for your success that you understand how to effectively use your voice.

In terms of effective use of your voice, you must consider the interactions of three key elements: i) volume ii) pace, speed and rhythm iii) pitch and tone. As a speaker, you can 'dial up' or 'dial down' any of these elements to create a specific mix that suits the content of that part of your presentation. By varying all three in different ways, you will create a dynamic and varied experience for your audience which will enable you to sustain their engagement level far longer. Picture control of these elements like the controls on a mixing desk:

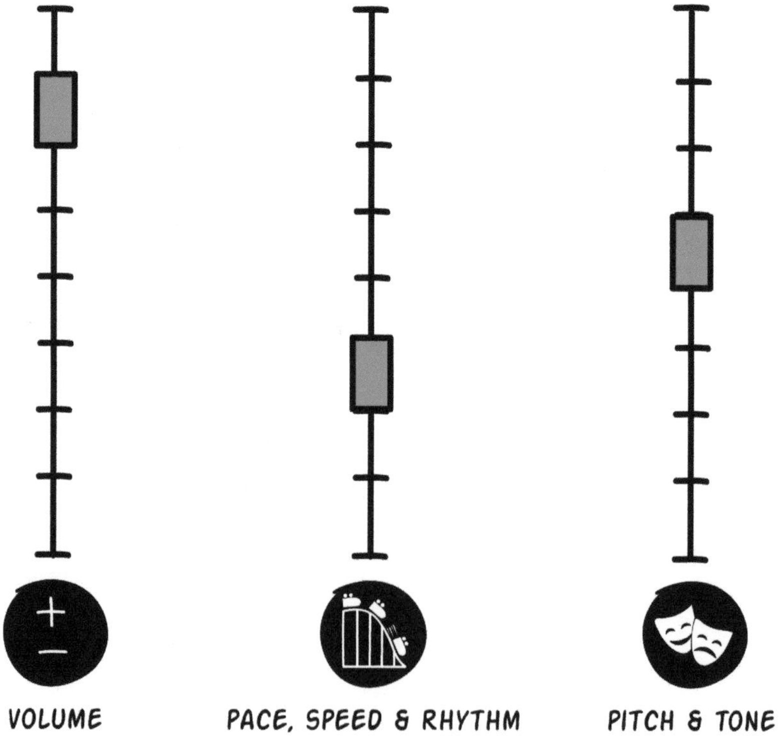

Here are three examples to illustrate the possibilities: If you want to say something personal to create a deeper connection with the audience you might speak quietly and slowly, and with emotion. If the subject is highly controversial, you might use a greater volume to show your confidence, a comfortable pace so you are clearly understood, and a less emotional tone to avoid displaying your own feelings. Finally, if the audience looks bored you might energise the group by increasing all three elements!

Volume

Naturally the volume required depends on the size and shape of the room you are in, but volume can be used more subtly for particular effects. It is important to use volume for emphasis and to hold your audience's attention by raising and lowering the volume of your delivery. Key words or ideas can be verbally 'highlighted' by increasing your volume. Many potentially good speakers fail to impress because they speak far too softly for too long. Speaking more loudly does more than increase your volume, it also increases your energy levels making you more animated and lively. As a result the audience is less likely to drift off and your message will be far clearer.

If you suffer with nerves and anxiety, a soft voice will reveal 'wobbles' in your tone and make you seem hesitant. Speaking with a loud clear voice 'smooths' your tone and gives the impression of great confidence. And that, as we know from chapter 2.2, will also make you *feel* more confident!

However, speaking loudly isn't the complete answer. If you **only** speak loudly the audience will find it tiring and you could become monotonous. Once you have captured your audience's attention, you can now have them on the edge of their seats by carefully lowering your voice - particularly if you are telling an interesting story or giving good advice. Contrasting a loud clear voice with a quiet, almost intimate tone is incredibly powerful and the change in dynamic will ensure the audience stays interested.

So, the key is to speak more loudly than feels comfortable to you, but ensure that you use both loud and soft tones to create impact and intimacy.

Pace, Speed and Rhythm

In recent decades, political speeches have taken on the features stereotypically characterised by American evangelist speakers. In this model, the speaker builds up speed and pace (often with volume) to a crescendo whilst whipping the audience up into an excitable frenzy! It's slightly disappointing to see this style become the modus operandi of so many people in the public spotlight because it is an unsubtle technique and not representative of best practice.

Despite this, many people still believe that by speaking more quickly they appear more dynamic. Actually, the real trick is not in the speed as such but rather the variation of speed and the rhythm.

You can do incredible things with the pacing and rhythm of your voice which, when mastered, are truly captivating.

Varying your speed makes for interesting listening and helps the audience maintain concentration. Broad messages can be covered at a faster tempo to generate energy and excitement. With complicated ideas, key messages, or technical information, it is more powerful to use a slow and deliberate pace. You could even slow your speech down to one word at a time.

Pitch and Tone

Whilst the other elements of your voice are very much under your conscious control, it is much harder to recognise and influence the pitch and tone of your voice. Pitch and tone refer more to the *emotional* content of your speech. Your speech will sound very different when you are angry to when you are happy. This is largely down to a 'tonal' change rather than purely your volume and pacing. When we communicate well, our speech is filled with feeling and emotion. Sadly all too often speakers use a flat, unemotional tone of voice which communicates nothing beyond the bare words.

The very best speakers ensure that when they talk, there is a clear emotional component to what they are saying.

A speech given at a single pace without variety of tone will quickly anaesthetise the audience. Your voice needs an ebb and flow, a rise and fall, to bring the sounds to life. Sometimes short staccato sentences create the right rhythm; at other times the words should flow as the emphasis requires.

Your speech will be most effective if you use all the elements covered in this section, varying them throughout your talk to create dynamic and emotional communication. Using any single technique without variation will become monotonous, no matter how well you use that technique.

How am I meant to get 'emotional' about my work? A lot of what I talk about is kinda dull!

It is easy to see how motivational speakers can get excited and passionate about their topics because their subjects are very emotive. In contrast, you could be forgiven for looking at your organisation and struggling to tap into strong feelings about these 'day to day' subjects. I'd like to challenge that assumption. Let's turn the question around: if you aren't able to show you care about your subject, how on earth do you expect your audience to care? As a speaker, your job is to encourage the audience to engage with the content. In order to achieve this, at the very least, you have to demonstrate some feeling towards whatever you're speaking about!

Perhaps you are benchmarking against the wrong emotions? High energy emotions are certainly difficult to manufacture for particular subjects. But there are a number of other, lower energy emotional words which I would expect any speaker to relate to:

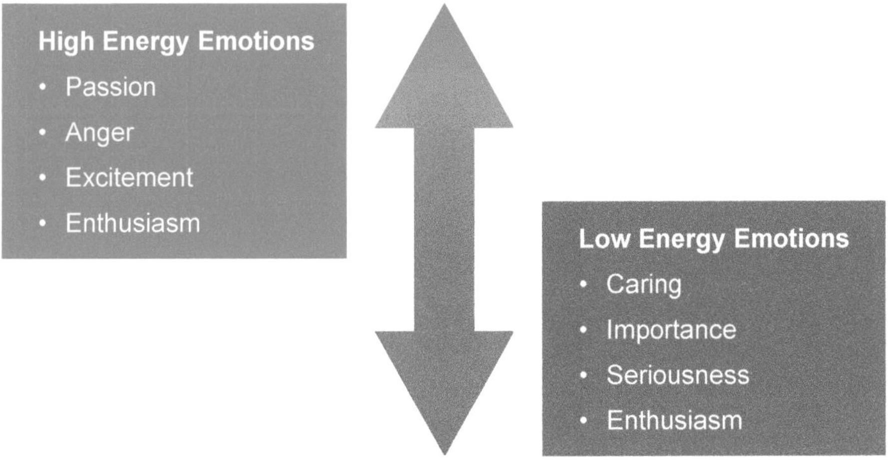

Enthusiasm features in both; it can manifest in the typical way you would expect to see it as demonstrated by a high energy motivational speaker, but it is an emotion that can just as easily manifest as a quiet eagerness to share content with the audience. You might not be passionate about the most recent financial audit results but you absolutely should be demonstrating that you care, that these results are important, that the topic is serious and that you are enthusiastic to speak about it. These are all emotions which I believe as a minimum standard you must be able to demonstrate when you speak.

2.6 Presenting alongside technology

Despite knowing all of these techniques, many presenters still fail to deliver with energy and to inspire their audience for one simple reason. It is probably the single biggest challenge you face in being truly engaging:

Knowing how to present alongside PowerPoint!

When you turn on technology you instantly take the audience's attention away from you, and no matter how great your slides are, they are very unlikely to motivate or inspire. Despite this, many speakers still believe that by investing time into the technology they can create slides that will perform this function. In my experience creating slides for a presentation takes up the vast majority of people's preparation time. Imagine the potential if, instead of using that time to create lots of slides, that time was spent preparing what to say and how to say it (using the process outlined in chapter 1.3). You would almost certainly end up with a more engaging presentation, with more interesting content and shorter, simpler slides that are easier to understand.

I'm not suggesting you abandon PowerPoint altogether; it certainly has a place. Consider, instead, 'adding it in' after you've mastered engaging an audience without it. Turning off the technology gives you the freedom to be yourself and is a refreshing change for your audience. Flipcharts and handouts can be used as effective replacements for slides.

Creating wonderfully visual slides with just the right amount of information is only the first hurdle. When using slides, there are a number of things which speakers and presenters routinely do that are unforgivable. A colleague once told me the following mistakes are the professional equivalent of wearing white socks with a black suit – you should just never do it!

What **NOT** to do!

The deadly sins of presenting alongside slides

DON'T STAND IN THE PROJECTOR BEAM

DON'T LET THE SLIDES TAKE CENTRE STAGE

DON'T LOOK AT THE SCREEN

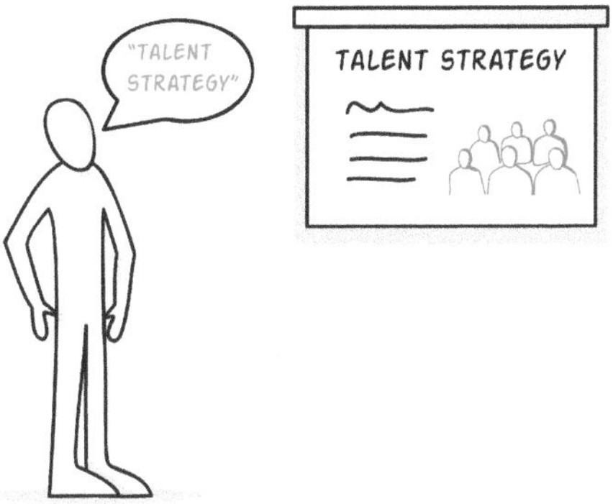

DON'T READ THE SLIDES

DON'T POINT THE REMOTE AT THE SCREEN WHEN YOU PRESS A BUTTON (...AND DON'T USE THE LASER!)

Standing in the beam

DON'T STAND IN THE PROJECTOR BEAM

Probably the most unforgivable of all presenting sins. I've lost count of the number of highly experienced and senior global business leaders I've seen standing with the projector beam across their face or body. Standing in the projector beam blocks the view of the screen, and the light shining in your face makes eye contact with the audience more challenging. But the biggest issue, by far, is that YOU LOOK LIKE AN IDIOT! You cannot maintain credibility when your slides are projected across your face/body.

Don't do it.

The problem usually occurs because projectors are placed in the centre of the room and, in order to maintain your presence in front of the audience, you end up moving into the beam. It's incredibly difficult to avoid when the projector is at table height, but a little easier when it's ceiling mounted. Obviously this doesn't apply if you are using a television, but since most meeting rooms are still fitted with projectors it's important to avoid this simple blunder.

The Solution

Learn the key on your keyboard that will make the screen blank and stop the beam. For most English language computers this is the 'b' key on the keyboard ('b' stands for black, thus on French language keyboards the key is 'n' for noir and so on). When the software is in presentation mode, pressing 'b' will turn the screen black, allowing you to stand where the projector beam had been. The additional benefit of this is that the audience's focus will instantly shift back to you the moment you blank the slideshow.

Note: Most presentation remotes will also have this function associated with one of the buttons.

Visit the chapter 2 resource section on the website for an example of the author making this **EXACT** mistake

Letting slides take centre stage

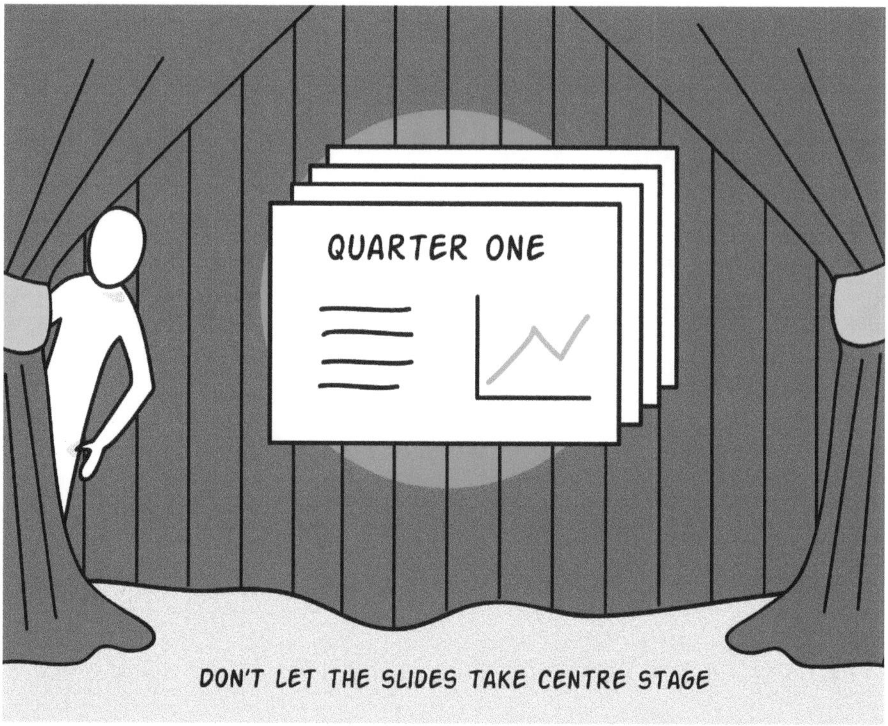
QUARTER ONE
DON'T LET THE SLIDES TAKE CENTRE STAGE

In over 90% of the meeting rooms I've been to, the presentation device has been fixed in the centre of the room with no option to move it. This is a spectacular mistake but few people in business have ever questioned it. As a result, room designers now believe it is the desired layout and it has therefore become the norm in meeting/training rooms worldwide. I cannot emphasise strongly enough how disastrous for engagement this simple design decision has been. Imagine this scenario: you walk into a meeting room to deliver a presentation (without slides) and find the flipchart placed right in the centre of the room. Would you move it? And if so, where to? My guess is that you would move the flipchart to the place where flipcharts always live in meeting/training rooms - just off to one side of the speaker, at the front of the room.

The reason you want to place flipcharts to one side of you is exactly the reason why you don't want slides to be at the centre of the room. The slides are there to support you, **NOT** to 'be the presentation'. You are the presentation. Unfortunately, by placing the technology centrally at the front of rooms we are forcing presenters into a difficult position. To avoid standing in the beam (my previous point), and in order to ensure all the audience can see the slides, presenters have to stand off to one side. There is an additional emotional implication to the practical problem: we know many presenters feel anxious about standing in front of an audience and this gives them the perfect excuse to stand either at the side of the room or, even worse, **BEHIND** the audience while narrating their slides. When a speaker is out of the spotlight in this way they tend to relax and forget they must still be present. All too often their delivery becomes a low energy, monotone narration of the material on the slides.

The Solution

There are two options: if possible, put the projector and the screen to your left or right hand side while you stand in the centre. When this isn't possible, you must ensure you still remain the main focus by standing confidently as close to the front as you can without being in the projector beam.

Don't forget you can use the 'b' button then move to the centre for a time.

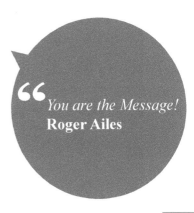

" *You are the Message!*
Roger Ailes

Talking to or looking at the slides

DON'T LOOK AT THE SCREEN

When we are anxious we are often afraid that we will forget what we want to say. In this context slides can be very reassuring to a presenter. However, we have already discussed the ways in which slides can both benefit and cause problems for your presentation by providing structure and direction. My concerns are that slides make a presenter less flexible and less able to respond to the needs of their audience. However, I see the advantages of having visual support to your structure and your flow of speech.

THIS DOES NOT MEAN YOU CAN USE SLIDES AS A TELEPROMPTER!

Teleprompters are the clever devices used by television presenters, professional speakers and politicians to read their script without the audience seeing. They are effective because they are invisible to the audience and, with practice, the presenter looks as if they are speaking naturally rather than reading from a script.

In most speaking or presenting situations, scripted presentations are less effective because natural speech is significantly more dynamic and engaging then written text read aloud. Turning around to look at your slides for cues, however, can be problematic.

Picture the scene: The speaker says, "Good morning, welcome to our session today. The first thing I want to discuss is..." - pause, clicks slides, looks at screen - "Ah yes, budget forecasting. This is a critical issue for the organisation and there are some important considerations..." - pause, clicks first bullet - "Right, okay, so firstly we have no standardised forecasting process..." We want to give the illusion that we know what we are saying, but instead we are actively showing that we need to read our own slides to prompt ourselves. Once again, credibility takes a nose dive!

Repeatedly looking at the screen for prompts makes the speaker look as if they don't know their material.

Even if you know your content inside out, the urge to turn and look at the screen is compelling and magnetic. There are also issues with audience engagement. Every time you glance behind you, you lose eye contact with your audience. Your energy levels will also drop as you process what is on the screen. Both these things shift your focus away from your audience and discourage engagement.

The Solution

Whenever possible, place your laptop in your forward line of sight as if it were part of the audience. You can then discreetly glance at the laptop in front of you rather than the screen behind you. I try to put my laptop next to, or close to, the audience so I can glance at it discreetly and naturally whilst I'm making eye contact with other audience members.

Sometimes you can be limited by the room layout. I always carry a 10 metre projector extension cable with me, so that even if the connection is behind me I am able to place my computer where I want it. It might seem excessive, but this small detail makes a huge impact on the audience and it's certainly worth the cost of an additional cable!

Reading from the slides

DON'T READ THE SLIDES

Almost certainly you knew this one was coming. It is probably the best known mistake made by presenters when using technology, and so it's a mystery to me why, despite knowing this, most presenters still end up doing it!! Quite honestly, if all you have to tell your audience is what's written on the slides, you may as well send them the slides and save everyone an unnecessary meeting. I think I've drilled home the message that you should never read the words that are on the screen. It adds no value to the audience, they can do that must faster than you and if you are speaking whilst they are reading they will retain less of the information.

This problem is the most widely cited and well documented feature of 'death by PowerPoint' and has become a standing joke in many organisations. When presenters start reading out a list of bullet points verbatim, you can physically feel the energy and engagement levels of the audience plummet! By reading from your slides you demonstrate a lack of creativity and skill, moreover you risk ridicule from your peers. Commit to doing better.

The Solution

- Be aware - if you find yourself reading from your slides, stop. Allow the audience time in silence to process the slide and then talk about the information on it, without reading it.
- Ditch the bullets – if you discuss your bullet points one at a time you will inevitably start reading from the slide. Try removing the bullets, keeping only the heading slide as your prompt. I've seen countless speakers transformed by this one simple change.
- If you must keep your bullet points, talk about the subject against a blank screen first before revealing the slide to summarise the key points you have discussed.
- Avoid writing 'natural conversation' sentences in your bullets - i.e. don't write it as you would say it. Keep only the key words to create a more powerful bullet, it doesn't have to be grammatically perfect (see the 6x6 rule in chapter 7.1). This avoids the temptation to 'read the text'. For example: "We need to review existing processes and consolidate what we find into a single process," becomes: "Review processes and consolidate."
- Use more images and fewer text sentences (again see chapter 7.1 for more on design tips).

Pointing the remote

DON'T POINT THE REMOTE AT THE SCREEN WHEN YOU PRESS A BUTTON (...AND DON'T USE THE LASER!)

It can be painful to watch a speaker walk back and forth to their computer to advance their slides. They look as if they are connected by an elastic band that keeps pulling them back.

To avoid this, presenters sometimes go a step further and simply stand next to their technology with their finger on the 'advance slide' button for their entire presentation. Both of these approaches look and feel unnatural and significantly affect the dynamism of the presentation.

You must always use a presentation remote so that you are free to move wherever you please and are not attached to your computer. These devices come in a number of different shapes and sizes; I recommend using the smallest, simplest design you can find. It needs to be easily held in your hand and preferably have a 'blank screen' button. More complex (and expensive) devices have an array of features. Whilst these can appear useful, in my experience they are more difficult to use and cause me to fumble with them or press the wrong buttons.

Most organisations provide a remote control in their meeting rooms, but this is no guarantee that a) you can find it in the cupboards and drawers of the room or b) it works. Most devices are made up of two parts: the remote and the receiver. The receivers are often small and easily lost so it's very easy for the two parts to become separated. There are also considerations about battery power and compatibility.

The Solution

I recommend buying your own presentation remote and keeping it with your computer. This way you can be confident that it works with your technology and that the batteries are charged. Select a small, simple device with the fewest possible buttons that takes a 'normal' sized, easily replaceable, battery.

But we haven't yet got to the sin...

NEVER point the remote at the screen when you press a button!! This drives me crazy. The screen and the remote are not connected, and the screen is most commonly a wall! If you want to point it at something, you should be aiming for the receiver attached to your computer, although presenters rarely do this. There is no need to '*point*' the device anywhere; thanks to modern technology the receiver will function perfectly well no matter what you do. Ideally your hands should be animated and expressive, and you should click when appropriate without any additional gestures or pointing. Curiously, men seem to be more susceptible to this sin than women. Perhaps they are reminded of childhood games involving toy guns because they display visible satisfaction from the power they can wield with this little device.

Side note: Most remotes will also have a laser pointer, but audiences tire very quickly of that little red dot darting around the screen. Use it sparingly or not at all.

CHAPTER SUMMARY

BODY-VOICE-WORDS

Although the statistics are not as straightforward as many people would have you believe, we know that body language and voice carry great weight for the audience. You must ensure that your gestures and vocal style mirror the content of the words. If there is a mismatch the audience will be more influenced by your body language and vocal tone rather than your words.

NERVES

Feeling anxious is a natural response to having a room of eyes on you! Nervousness can take many forms, so it is important that you recognise your unique reaction and learn techniques to manage it. Find environments such as cinemas, theatres or local groups where you can practise becoming more comfortable being looked at.

HANDS AND FEET

Practise the parking position until it feels natural to you. Feet shoulder width apart, hips in the middle, hands by your sides. It will feel very unusual at first but it looks the strongest. Only once you have mastered it can you think about putting movement into your presentation style.

For references and links from this chapter visit chris-atkinson.co.uk/books

EYE CONTACT AND PAUSE

Both eye contact and pausing should be held just beyond what feels comfortable. Typically this is a slow count to three. Eye contact should be made with one person at a time, don't work in a pattern but do aim to connect individually with each person. Move on once you see an acknowledgement of the connection. Pausing after a key point is essential; hold eye contact while pausing.

VOICE

Consistency is the enemy of vocal impact. Anything you do in the same way, for too long, will start to be filtered out by the audience members' brains. For that reason, you must vary your tone, volume and speed throughout your presentation.

TECHNOLOGY

Remember slides are the biggest risk to you being engaging and inspiring. Many speakers turn in to boring drones once the slides come on. Try to put the projector to one side of you so you can stay in the centre of the room. Keep out of the projector beam and don't turn around to read from the screen.

2

CHAPTER

3

CREATING GROUP ENGAGEMENT

Now we've covered the core elements of presenting, hopefully you are feeling more confident and ready to set yourself apart from the crowd! Most business people rely on a one-way presentation style using slides to 'lecture' their audience which, as we know, will commonly result in extreme boredom. This chapter covers techniques you can use to involve your audience in the subject matter and encourage interaction. Not only will your audience be far more engaged, they will also retain more of the material presented and are far more likely to demonstrate a meaningful change in behaviour.

3.1 The definition and facts behind engagement

There are many definitions and measures of engagement. The most widely accepted definition of employee engagement was created by a group of psychologists at Utrecht University. They defined employee engagement as a measure of three things:

1. Energy and vigour
2. Dedication
3. Absorption

In other words, engaged employees have a sense of an energetic and effective connection with their work, they show dedication and will persist with tasks to the best of their abilities, and they will 'lose themselves' in their tasks, often finding great satisfaction from that absorption. The two best known measures come from Gallup in the form of their Q12[24] and Utrecht University with their Utrecht Work Engagement Scale (UWES)[25].

As we covered in the introduction, the data coming from these measurement tools is creating a significant cultural change across organisations. Over a three-year period Gallup surveyed 350,000 employees from a diverse range of industry sectors. The results of this survey published in 2013, ***State of***

the American Workplace,[26] sent shockwaves across the world. The report stated: *"these latest findings indicate that 70% of American workers are 'not engaged' or 'actively disengaged' and are emotionally disconnected from their workplaces and less likely to be productive."* You read that correctly - 70%! The figure is so startling, so unbelievable, that it fuelled a huge interest in this topic of 'engagement'. Gallup estimated that of the people in the "actively disengaged" category alone (18% of the total population) the cost to the U.S. is somewhere between $450 billion and $550 billion each year in lost productivity. The report concludes that this group *"are more likely to steal from their companies, negatively influence their co-workers, miss workdays, and drive customers away."*

If you are living outside of America I'm sure you're wondering if perhaps your country might be different. Perhaps you feel 'surely we must do better than that!' Fortunately (or not, as you will see), Gallup's 2013 ***State of the Global Workplace***[27] has that question covered. The study surveyed 142 countries and 74,000 employees. The report concluded: "*The bulk of employees worldwide - 63% - are 'not engaged,' meaning they lack motivation and are less likely to invest discretionary effort in organisational goals or outcomes. And 24% are 'actively disengaged,' indicating they are unhappy and unproductive at work and liable to spread negativity to co-workers. In rough numbers, this translates into 900 million not engaged and 340 million actively disengaged workers around the globe."*[28]

If any of this is surprising to you then don't worry, you are not alone. A research report by *The Economist,* **Re-engaging with engagement,** surveyed 331 senior level executives in Europe and the Middle East. Almost half surveyed were board level and the rest were senior directors. The report concluded: "*Executives consistently held a 'rose-tinted' view of engagement that is not shared lower down the ranks. Senior managers pay for engagement surveys and make superficial adjustments, but they don't really believe in people. If they did, they would fundamentally change the way they operate."* [29]

The assumption of many organisations is that the issues of disengagement can be addressed through policy changes, new incentives or reward schemes. Unfortunately, most people have fundamentally misunderstood the question '*where and when does engagement happen?'* The answer to 'where it happens' is **everywhere** and 'when it happens' is **every day**. Ultimately, engagement characterises the relationship between an employee and their organisation. Far from the commonplace assumption that engagement is an organisational and cultural issue (i.e. high level and big picture), the truth is far simpler and more profound. The responsibility for creating engagement must lie primarily with the day-to-day leaders and managers of employees - the people who stand in front of teams and give direction, training or guidance. In other words, YOU! It is your responsibility (and your challenge) to actively engage your colleagues whenever you speak to or work with them.

In chapter 1.4 we learnt about the primacy and recency effects. We know that, as a presenter you are 'gifted' a higher level of engagement at the start and at the end of your delivery, and you need to capitalise on that time to create a powerful and long lasting positive impact.

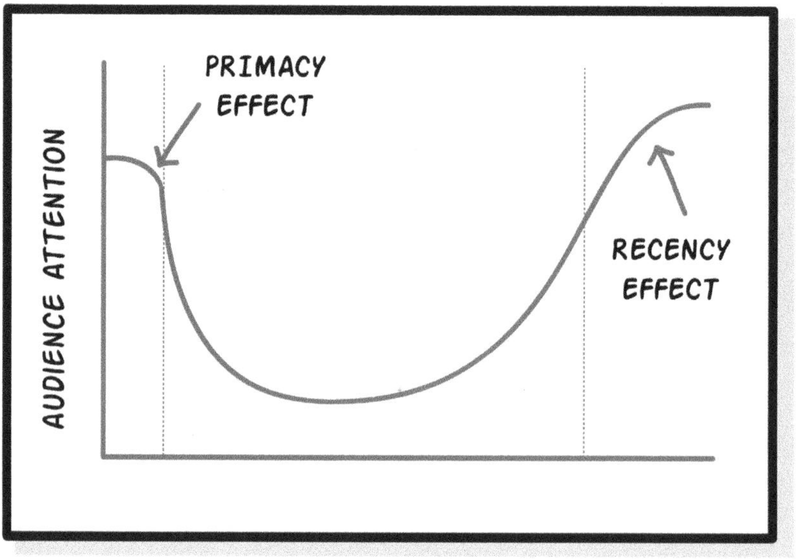

However, we didn't address the giant gap in the middle! This dip in audience attention is inevitable unless you take action to counteract it. It is essential to sustain engagement with energising activities and conversation to prevent the audience's attention drifting away. This isn't about silly distractions or icebreakers; it is about making the audience engage with each of your key points so the content and learning sticks! The rest of this chapter is packed with ideas to get your audiences and your team members fully engaged so your content will be remembered.

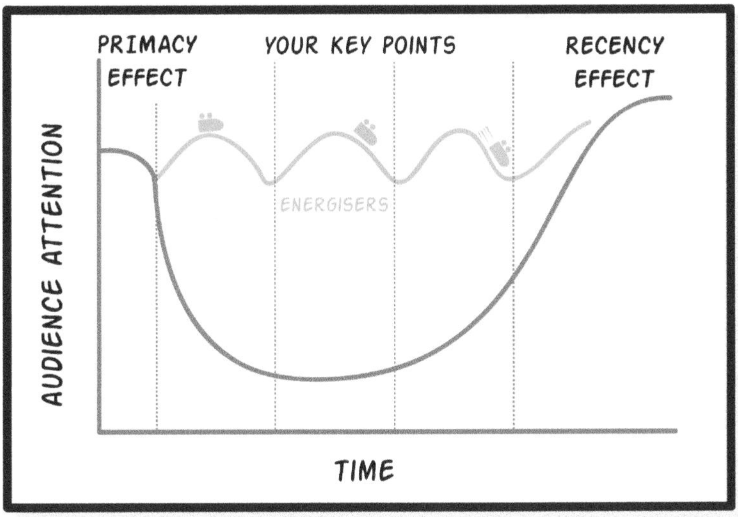

You can create a more dynamic pacing by adding energisers throughout your communication. Think of it like a rollercoaster: a topic's importance is similar to a rollercoaster inching up a big slope. You can use more serious, reflective activities, which have a higher level of intensive focus and thought. Just as a rollercoaster releases the tension of the slow climb by zooming down the other side of the slope, it is important that you release the tension of this intensive work for your audience. You can use lighter, faster-paced activities. Group activities that generate energy and ideas work well here.

3.2 Multiple intelligence theory

The increasing popularity of Neuro Linguistic Programming[30] has familiarised us with the three general categories in which people learn: visual learners, auditory learners, and kinaesthetic (physical) learners. Beyond these three general categories, however, there have been many theories of human potential. The one that I have found most useful for driving audience engagement is the theory of multiple intelligences, developed by Howard Gardner PhD, Professor of Education at Harvard University.

Gardner's early work in psychology, and later in human potential, led to the development of the initial six intelligences. He was one of the first people to question judging people on their I.Q. which he considered to be a narrow definition of intelligence. He proposed that everybody's mind is different and no two profiles of 'intelligence' are the same. Since his initial work, this concept has been developed and additional intelligences are often discussed in academic literature. For our purposes, the original eight are the most useful.

Verbal-Linguistic Intelligence

This represents well-developed sensitivity to the sounds and meanings of words as well as a love of both spoken and written language. This commonly looks like a love of reading, writing and speaking.

Logical-Mathematical Intelligence

The ability to think both conceptually and abstractly. In addition to numerical ability such as mathematics this intelligence also includes the capacity to notice and develop logical relationships and patterns. This commonly looks like strength in working quickly with numbers or recognising and identifying patterns.

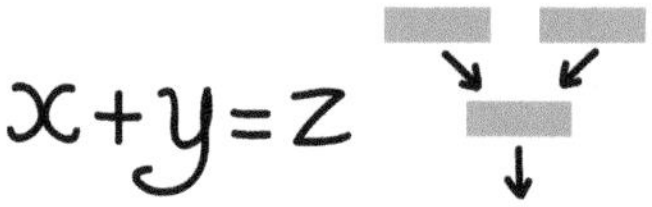

Spatial-Visual Intelligence

The capacity to think in images and pictures, to visualise both accurately and abstractly. In addition to pictorial information this could also include a strong awareness of physical space, shape and size. This commonly looks like a love of images, pictures, charts as well as being able to accurately judge special dimensions.

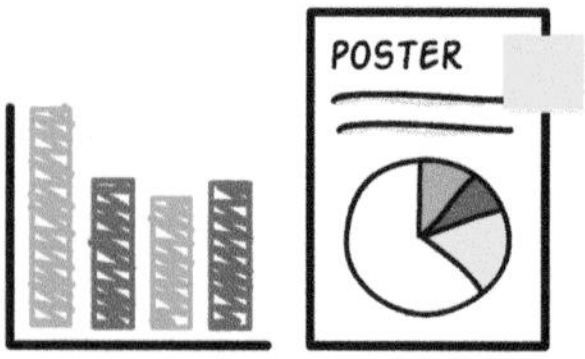

Bodily-Kinaesthetic Intelligence

This is the ability to handle objects skilfully and in particular to understand things primarily through touch. This commonly looks like a need to hold something, investigate or manipulate it in order to get a clear understanding of it.

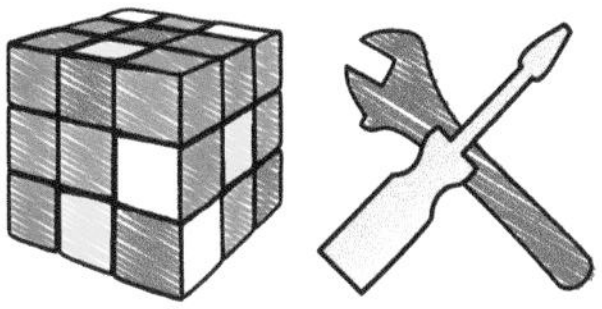

Musical Intelligence

The ability to produce and appreciate rhythm, pitch and timbre. It is not restricted to the ability to play musical instruments but rather to have a strong relationship to sound and rhyme. This commonly looks like a love of music, dislike of discordant sounds and creation of rhymes to remember things.

Interpersonal Intelligence

Learning through discussion with others and social interaction with other people. This commonly looks like a love of debate, discussion and talking through issues with others.

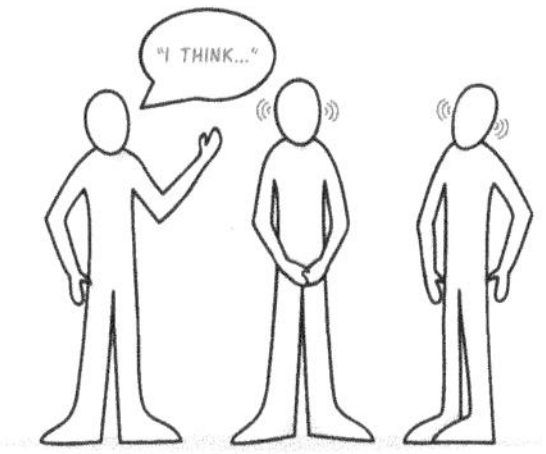

Intrapersonal Intelligence

Learning through reflection and private thought. This intelligence is about being self-aware and in tune with feelings, values, beliefs and thinking processes. This commonly looks like a need to have personal space to first reflect, think and process information before discussing or making decisions.

Naturalistic Intelligence

The ability to recognise, relate to and understand the natural world. It also encompasses a strong intuitive understanding of how the world works and common sense. This commonly looks like a love of being outdoors, natural light and being around animals.

If we want to engage a group of people, Gardner's model of multiple intelligences gives us a useful template to structure a range of activities and exercises that appeal to the different profiles. When I'm designing an activity to engage my audience this is always my starting point.

If you are curious about your own preferences, there is a short self-assessment which you can download from the website. The answers will reveal where your preferences lie and what areas you might be inclined to overlook! It's important to note that when designing activities for a group you need to put your own style and preferences to one side and focus on blending as many of the intelligences together as possible. The following chapters will look at ways to do this.

3.3 How to involve your audience

In chapter 3.1 we looked at the concept of energisers - activities that connect your audience with the content. These don't have to be elaborate; the simplest things can be hugely powerful. Consider the humble post-it note (other brands of sticky note are available). When used creatively this simple piece of stationery can transform a discussion into a high-energy participative activity which stimulates many of the intelligences.

Scenario 1: Running a team meeting to create a plan for the upcoming 12 months

1. "On your own, think about what you believe our priorities should be for the next 12 months" - **Intrapersonal intelligence**
2. "In small groups, share your thoughts with your colleagues and write down all of your ideas on post-it notes, one idea per sticky note (no duplication)" - **Interpersonal and verbal linguistic intelligence**
3. "Stand up and scatter your sticky notes over the wall/flipchart etc" - **Bodily kinaesthetic intelligence**
4. "Looking at all the ideas, start to group them into common themes" - **Spatial-visual, bodily kinaesthetic and logical mathematical intelligence**
5. "For each grouping, create a label or name that encapsulates the theme of that group" - **Verbal linguistic intelligence**
6. "In private, take a moment to reflect on the groups. Which do you feel should be our top 3 priorities? In what order?" - **Intrapersonal intelligence**
7. Group discussion follows!

This could have been a meeting about a typically boring subject such as strategy or planning, densely packed with slides and delivered as a 'tell' from senior management. Instead, by inviting the employees to participate, we've created a lively conversation between the people who are directly involved with the subject. Because the participants generated the content of the meeting they will feel ownership of it, increasing their accountability as well as their engagement. All we used were some post-it notes and a bit of creative thought around multiple intelligences.

Let's add in a couple more ideas and develop another scenario. Policy changes, regulatory updates or legal issues are inevitably delivered as a 'tell'. Generally it is assumed this type of subject matter is not appropriate for 'engagement'. The result is that the speaker lectures the group and ends their talk with 'any questions?', to which there is silence. The audience leaves, bored, having absorbed very little. The presenter assumes the audience understood since there were no questions. It is a total waste of time.

Scenario 2: Release of new government regulation affecting your industry

1. Create a multiple choice quiz about the topic where the answers explore less well known data about your company, your customers, existing regulation and so on - **Logical mathematical intelligence**

2. Run the quiz, asking participants to move to corners of the room according to their answer (a,b,c,d) - **Bodily kinaesthetic and intrapersonal (if answering individually) intelligence**

3. Emphasise how easy it is to assume we know the information or how inconsistent knowledge is within the organisation (or whatever is revealed by the way the group answer) – **Linguistic intelligence**

4. Hand out the new regulation document and highlighters. Ask audience to read the text highlighting anything they think is very important/relevant or anything they have a question about - **Linguistic and intrapersonal intelligence**

5. In small groups discuss what they highlighted and capture on sticky notes/flipchart most important areas and any questions - **Interpersonal and verbal linguistic intelligence**

6. Whole group discussion debating the points raised by each group and answering questions – **Interpersonal, logical mathematical and verbal linguistic intelligence**

7. Difficult or ambiguous scenarios activity – create two or three scenarios in which the actions to be taken are somewhat ambiguous or judgement based (i.e. no correct answer; this makes the activity very engaging). The groups discuss how they would handle these situations followed by whole group debrief of each scenario – **Interpersonal, intrapersonal, logical mathematical and verbal linguistic intelligence**

Once again, with nothing other than some basic stationery and creative thought we have turned a potentially uninspiring topic into a highly energised discussion which is far more likely to be remembered and applied.

Designing activities like this to replace a delivered presentation may sound simple, but it can be tricky to ensure your topics are addressed in a direct and meaningful way. You need time to practise and to clarify exactly how you want it to work. Using something as simple as a post-it note requires a certain level of thought; there is a depth and subtlety even in this one small tool (see chapter 7.2 for correct sticky note usage!).

In both scenarios you may have noticed the absence of two of Gardner's intelligences – musical and naturalistic. Whilst these two are interesting and valuable, they require a certain creativity to use effectively in a business context. Here are a few ways that I manage to incorporate them into sessions.

Musical Intelligence

- Have music playing before the session, during breaks etc.
- If our company/team/product was a genre of music what would it be?
- What chart song title captures the essence of this subject?
- Create a rhyme or song to help remember the key points

Naturalistic Intelligence

- Ensure you get as much natural daylight into the room as possible by fully opening blinds etc.
- Ask participants to get fresh air in coffee breaks
- When problem solving look at parallels in nature for inspiration, "how is this problem solved in the natural world?"
- Go offsite – change your environment walk and talk!

Here are some ideas for the remaining six:

Verbal-Linguistic Intelligence

- Ask lots of questions and facilitate discussion
- Give handouts and further reading
- Ask participants to write ideas on flipcharts
- Participants prepare and deliver a presentation

Logical-Mathematical Intelligence

- Quizzes, brain teasers, puzzles etc.
- Make new or logical connections between subjects
- Categorise and organise information
- Create sequences, flow or processes
- Solve problems

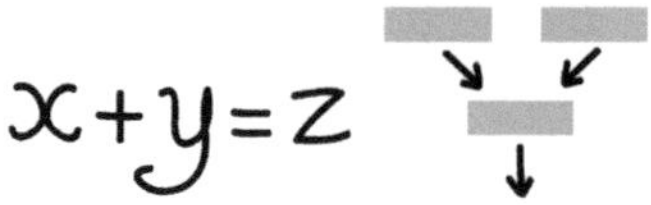

Spatial-Visual Intelligence

- Use images and pictures
- Use diagrams to explain your content
- Put all flipcharts and sticky notes used in the session on the walls (decorate the room with all content created)
- Take photographs of the session and content to circulate afterwards
- Visual aids can be printed posters or slides

SPATIAL-VISUAL INTELLIGENCE

Bodily-Kinaesthetic Intelligence

- Use props such as models or prototypes
- Give out sticky notes, marker pens, Blu-Tack etc.
- Throw (soft) objects between people
- Find ways to have the audience move around the room
- Audience build or create something tangible

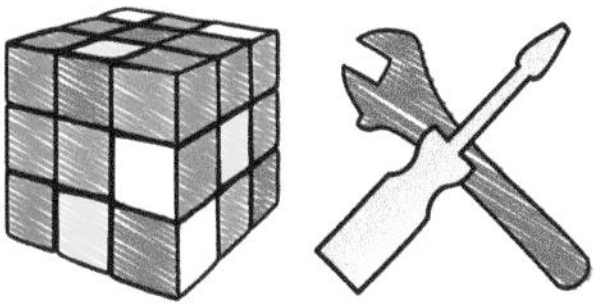

Interpersonal Intelligence

- Discuss topics as a whole group and in smaller groups
- Peer coaching and feedback
- Debate and play devil's advocate
- Prepare and present information

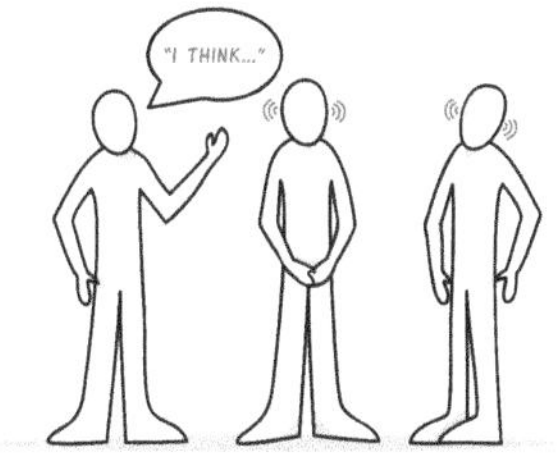

Intrapersonal Intelligence

- Assessments or self-assessments
- Private research time and advance assignments
- Write blogs
- Private reflection time

Having established the value of the multiple intelligence theory, I'm now going to be somewhat controversial: it is irrelevant to our purposes whether the theory of multiple intelligences is valid or not! This is because the single biggest hurdle most people face in this area is creativity. Gardener's model is so useful because it provides a framework for focussing creative thought. Generally, if someone sits down with a clean piece of paper and pen, their mind will go blank. Without creative thought, they are likely to open up PowerPoint and start creating slides. With Gardner's model, however, all you need to do is slowly work through it, ticking off the various intelligences. The more you tick off the more engaging and creative your session is likely to be. If you find yourself lacking in creative thought, examine which intelligences you have used and which are missing (i.e. I need something intrapersonal, what private reflective activity can I get people to do?).

Irrespective of your opinions on the theory, you will find that this methodology creates wonderfully varied and enjoyable sessions for your participants.

A NOTE OF CAUTION

The best activities are often the ones that are simplest and easiest for the audience to engage with. Although I am encouraging you to be creative, be very careful not to make your ideas overly complex and convoluted. If the audience gets confused or misunderstands you then their engagement level will drop and they will quickly become frustrated. Test out your instructions on a few volunteers before you run the activity. You will often find your instructions can be interpreted in different ways and this will enable you to clarify them.

In my two example scenarios, each instruction links to just one or two intelligences and is carefully explained step by step rather than in one long complex list. Getting the balance right in this way is an art form and takes practice..

3.4 Using props and technology to create impact

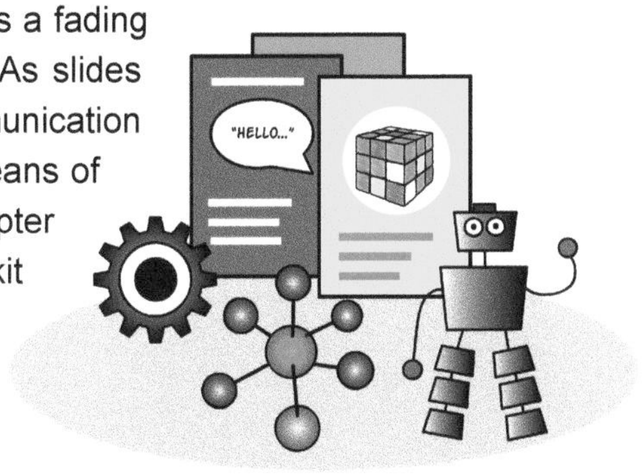

The use of props to create impact is a fading art and I think this is a huge loss. As slides increasingly dominate our communication we have lost sight of alternative means of presenting information. In this chapter I refer to props, stationery and kit as 'technology' because this is the technology of an engaging speaker. Slides are not the only technology you can employ. Chapter 7 covers this subject in depth and provides examples of the other non-digital presenting technologies available.

When you are creating your presentation, always think about how you can bring the content from the digital world into the real world. In other words, find ways to transpose the ideas on your screen into things your audience can physically see or touch. For example, use models of products or prototypes, or bring along actual machinery, components or tools. All of these things will appeal to the bodily kinaesthetic people as well as being generally interesting!

You can also think in terms of *analogy*. Your use of props does not need to be literal; you can use props which illustrate an analogy to your subject matter. Think about what other everyday object or experience is similar to your topic. If you are running a creativity session about how to grab the attention of passers-by at a recruitment fair, you might hand out cereal boxes and ask your audience to assess how the boxes are designed to grab attention (or glossy magazines and so on). If you are talking about teamwork, you could introduce various pieces of sporting equipment to prompt discussion about how different types of team work together to perform most effectively. Finally, you can use posters and illustrations. This may seem unnecessary or wasteful, but a printed poster is considerably more memorable and interesting to an audience than a slide which is shown for just a few seconds. Digital information is perceived as transient; tangible information holds more weight and will be remembered for much longer.

Be brave and find or create props to bring along to the session to facilitate discussion. It is more engaging for your audience and it shows the thought you have put into your presentation. Which links us neatly into our next subject, showmanship...

3.5 Using showmanship techniques

> *This is the day of dramatisation. Merely stating a truth isn't enough. The truth has to be made vivid, interesting, dramatic. You have to use showmanship. The movies do it. Television does it. And you will have to do it if you want attention.* **Dale Carnegie**

This sounds very relevant to our world doesn't it? Our attention span seems so short these days. We're surrounded by technology bombarding us with messages, to the point where our minds are saturated and content rarely sticks. Advertisers and speakers alike have recognised that we are living in the age of dramatisation – if we don't stand out we probably won't be remembered! It might surprise you to learn, then, that the quote above is from Dale Carnegie's book ***How to Win Friends and Influence People***[31]**,** written in 1936. All that time ago, Carnegie recognised that it was increasingly difficult for a speaker or an organisation to get the attention of an audience because of the rapid growth in communications. He dedicated the rest of his life to training others in the art of effective communication. Central to his teaching was the importance of standing out from the crowd; namely, the art of showmanship.

Showmanship techniques can potentially bring the greatest rewards, but they come with the greatest risk. Good use of showmanship can set you apart as an outstanding presenter and make you charismatic and memorable. But showmanship takes time, planning and practice – you cannot make it up as you go along. If this is new to you, don't be intimidated, but do approach these techniques with care. In time, your confidence will grow along with your ambitions, until you are delivering memorably and with impact.

Showmanship is defined simply as "the skill of performing in such a manner that will appeal to an audience."[32]

For our purposes, when I refer to showmanship I am also incorporating Dale Carnegie's idea of dramatisation. Showmanship is doing something dramatic to get the attention of an audience for the purpose of making a key point. Many speakers feel intimidated by the prospect of showmanship because they think of magicians and stage performers who are, undoubtedly, masters of the craft. Showmanship can be far simpler than this, however, and is one of the most accessible techniques you can use to make yourself memorable. Here are some simple examples I've seen over the years:

A leader brought a large pneumatic drill to a session on health and safety to dramatise the number of different ways he could injure himself with the tool – that is showmanship!
A speaker, discussing ways to save utility costs, burned real money in front of the audience. As it happens it set off the fire alarm and caused a full site evacuation... but that aside – that is showmanship!
A lawyer took off his suit jacket, tie and shirt in front of the audience (initially causing concern) to emphasise the point that he is more than just his role, and that we need to build a relationship with the person not just their function – that is showmanship!
An IT trainer asked all participants to write down their name and date of birth on pieces of card. Once he'd collected their details he listed all the private things he could access online if he were a hacker, using just this information. At the end he made a visible point of shredding all the cards – that is showmanship!
A salesman, demonstrating the strength of his product, unexpectedly produced a hammer and hit his product loudly. The audience assumed he'd smashed it but the product showed no noticeable damage – that is showmanship!

These are not huge, over the top things to do, nor do they require the stage presence of a master magician. In each example a message was given clearly and memorably through dramatisation, using showmanship simply but effectively. The fact that I still remember these events so many years later is testament to the power of showmanship and demonstrates exactly why you should invest thought in this area. I must have listened to thousands of presentations, and the ones that consistently stand out in my mind are the ones that had an element of showmanship.

To this end, early in my career I attended a magic workshop to learn some simple magic tricks and illusions that I could use to dramatise my key messages.

A handful of techniques from this course catapulted my impact instantly. I certainly had to learn to be bolder with my presentation style in order to use these new elements but the feedback I started receiving was much more powerful. Audience members and participants started advising their colleagues to come on my training programmes, and a number of organisations asked specifically for me by name to deliver programmes for them. In addition, through using these techniques my self-confidence, boldness and creativity as a speaker grew significantly. To this day it was the best investment in my own personal development that I have ever made.

Once you have grasped some simple showmanship techniques and have experimented at that level, you may be ready for more advanced ideas. This is where the practice and preparation comes in. If you master this technique you have a good chance of going viral! By that I mean everyone in your organisation will be talking about it, and if it's caught on camera you may even find online fame. Unfortunately, failure can be a painfully embarrassing experience and I've experienced this first-hand many times - usually when attempting magic tricks to explain learning points to an audience. Each embarrassing failure has helped me along this journey and I've learnt from each mistake, ensuring they are not repeated. With persistence and practice it will work well and will appear effortless to your audience.

British businessman Richard Branson is something of a legend when it comes to showmanship. His acts of showmanship have maintained his down to earth, fun and charismatic reputation. Here are just a few:

- To publicise the launch of his retail store Virgin Brides, he shaved off his trademark beard and wore a wedding dress and full makeup.
- When Virgin launched Virgin Cola he drove a tank down Fifth Avenue in New York City and through Times Square, where he pretended to blow up the Coca-Cola sign.
- After losing a bet with AirAsia CEO Tony Fernandes over each company's Formula 1 racing teams, Branson served as a female flight attendant (dressed accordingly) on an AirAsia aeroplane.
- He wore a spacesuit to the press conference for Virgin Galactic.
- Branson celebrated the first Virgin America flight by bungee jumping off the Palms Hotel Casino in Las Vegas, a 407 foot tall building. The stunt did not go quite as planned, and Branson crashed against the building twice and ripped his trousers.

Maybe this says something about the airline industry, but South West Airline's CEO Herb Keller is also famous for his charismatic acts of showmanship. Most famously, in an attempt to avoid a lawsuit with another aviation company over the motto "Just Plane Smart," Herb challenged the CEO of the other company to an arm wrestling match to settle the issue.[33] The video of this match went viral, and it is sometimes billed as the greatest publicity stunt ever.

You can take inspiration from such flamboyant acts but, as always, I caution against mimicry. It is better to take an idea that appeals to you and make it your own. If Branson's penchant for dressing up triggers an idea for you perhaps you could find something appropriate for your organisation – wearing hugely inappropriate clothing for a health and safety talk for example, or dressing in body armour to discuss handling difficult negotiations. I'm **not** suggesting you have to drive a tank, arm wrestle the competition or rappel down the side of a building in order to be a great showman! Rather that you can take inspiration from the spirit behind these things, and there are great rewards for taking that risk.

Search YouTube for these videos:

1. 'Rapping Flight Attendant from Southwest Airlines' – this flight attendant realised that very few passengers pay attention to the preflight safety briefings, so he decided to make it more memorable with a wonderful act of showmanship.
2. 'April Fools Video Prank in Math Class' – this lecturer clearly went to great efforts to create a fantastically memorable and unexpected moment that his students (and now the world!) will never forget.

These are examples of ordinary people who took the time and care to do sometime extraordinary. You too can be extraordinary, with a little thought and a lot of courage!

Tip:

Move swiftly on following any act of showmanship; you will maintain the pace and, if it was badly received, it will avoid embarrassment. In other words 'don't milk it'!

Dos and don'ts of showmanship

What to do:	What to avoid:
• Be 'big' and exude confidence • Smile • Practise practise practise • Create your own 'patter' that links closely with the subject at hand • Keep ideas simple - look for inspiration in your organisational environment and in corporate materials	• Seeking applause • Too much 'flare' or pizazz • Showmanship with no purpose – you must explain how your stunt is relevant to the subject you are discussing • Big-headed showing-off

So in summary, to be successful with your showmanship you must be bold, big, and deliver with huge enthusiasm. Don't look for or expect applause; this is about doing something unusual and innovative, not about being a one man show.

3.6 Telling jokes and anecdotes

I'd like you to think about this question openly and honestly:

Do people spontaneously, and without prompting, tell you that you are funny?

If you answered with something along the lines of 'yes, people often remark that I'm a funny person. They tell me spontaneously, without me pressurising them into saying it', then you are one of the few fortunate people in the world who I would recommend tell jokes during a presentation. If, however, your answer is more along the lines of 'well no, no one has actually *told* me directly that I'm funny but people often laugh at my jokes', then I'm afraid you, like the rest of us, should avoid joke telling.

The thing is, the ability is tell jokes is largely binary. You can't be 'somewhat' good at joke telling. Some people have a natural ability to time a joke; they know how to build it up and deliver it in a way that gets a positive response. Those people will be frequently told by others, quite directly, that they are a funny person. I accept that it is possible, with practice, to learn the art of telling jokes, but my instinct is that it's unlikely you will be successful. For those of us who are not regularly told we are funny, there is a more practical alternative discussed later in this chapter.

Jokes

It might seem like a good idea to use jokes because smiles and laughter can help you quickly build a rapport with an audience, but in reality this is rather difficult to achieve. The problem is, humour is subjective and it is nearly impossible to find a joke that amuses everybody. So when you tell a joke, you are appealing to the people who laugh at it but, crucially, you are putting off the people who don't find it funny. If you are determined to use a joke in your presentation, make sure it has a very broad appeal and consistently makes people laugh when you tell it.

It is helpful for a joke to be short because a long build up could lead to disappointment. Also, it goes without saying that you should avoid anything that could be considered inappropriate (and when it comes to humour, that excludes about 90% of jokes!). Most importantly, at the end of the joke make sure to quickly and smoothly link the content of the joke with the content of the session – don't wait for the laugh! As with acts of showmanship, the more quickly you move on the better it will look.

Jokes are high risk: only a handful of people can pull them off and even then not all of the audience will relate to the humour. However, you can still become the funny person you'd like to be and use humour to your advantage using another technique: **the anecdote**.

Anecdotes

When we tell an anecdote based on personal experience, we speak very differently to the way we speak when we're reciting memorised text or factual information. We speak more authentically and intimately, and in a world heavily sanitised by business speak and corporate language this can be incredibly refreshing for the audience. I'll discuss the importance of authenticity in greater detail in chapter 4.2.

Light hearted anecdotes are an absolute gift to speakers and have many advantages:

i) you don't need to memorise anything since you are just recalling something that happened

ii) you will speak more naturally because you're talking about a real experience

iii) audiences love stories and, importantly, *love* light hearted stories (see chapter 4.4 for more on storytelling techniques and methodologies)

You might be thinking 'I can't think of any amusing anecdotes!' This is the response I usually get when I approach this subject, but this couldn't be further from the truth. You may believe your life hasn't been that interesting and that tales of your experiences will not engage and entertain an audience. In fact, your life has been filled with wonderfully entertaining situations... just not always entertaining for you!

Invariably, the best anecdotes are the ones in which something has gone horribly wrong for you. At the time, you undoubtedly regretted the decisions that led you to that point, but these embarrassing events from your past now provide you with valuable material. Telling a great anecdote about an embarrassing situation more than makes up for the horror you felt when it was happening!

An international metal packaging company once asked me to speak in Switzerland to their executive team about engaging leadership. I spent several days preparing for this talk because the success of my presentation would dictate the future direction of my work with a particular division. The client had flown me to Zurich to present to the head office and most of the senior team, and on the morning of my presentation I entered the room feeling strong and confident. I had taken great care to look smart and had even purchased a new suit for the occasion. I was alone in the room for a few minutes whilst the audience were getting coffee and breakfast just outside the meeting room. I bent down to plug in my laptop and... my trousers ripped. Not a small tear either - they ripped all the way from the back just below my belt, through the crotch and right to the front where the zip was. My audience was just outside of the room waiting to come in, I had only brought the one suit with me and the clothes I'd travelled in were in no way suitable to change into. Despite all my preparation and my previous confidence, I suddenly felt extremely self-conscious and anxious. All I could do was button up my jacket and hope that this might conceal the damage. For the entire presentation I stood very still with my knees together, and avoided any large movements that might lift the jacket and reveal the 'situation'. I worked hard to animate my voice and facial expressions and maintain audience eye contact, but I am certain that I must have looked rather strange and far less animated than usual!

That is certainly one of the most embarrassing things that has happened to me as a speaker. I was mortified and I didn't tell anybody about it for a long time. But, as time passed, I gained some perspective and realised it was a wonderfully entertaining story for other people to hear because it exemplifies the difficulties a speaker might experience. It also shows, I hope, that I have had ups and downs on my journey to being a great speaker. I frequently use this anecdote when I'm talking to audiences about presentation skills.

Scan back through your experiences; cast your mind back to the start of your career, your days in education or your awkward early teenage years. You will certainly find plenty of stories you could use. The art is in selecting an anecdote that is suitable for your subject matter and for your particular audience. As with joke telling, move swiftly and smoothly from your anecdote to the link connecting it to the subject of your presentation.

There is one cardinal rule to the use of anecdotes:
Only ever use true stories from your personal experience.

Additional guidelines:

- Don't ever make up a story
- Avoid telling third party stories ("a friend once told me…")
- Don't exaggerate the anecdote
- Avoid anecdotes where the humour is at someone else's expense
- Don't try to be funny - let the story reveal the humour
- Avoid anecdotes that could genuinely damage your reputation

CHAPTER SUMMARY

ENGAGEMENT

Engagement is not a 'soft' subject. It is directly correlated to business and personal performance. We know that audience attention dips in the middle of presentations, just as the speaker is introducing the key points, so you need to plan energisers to engage the audience during this period.

MULTIPLE INTELLIGENCES

For our purposes multiple intelligence theory is simply a way to access creativity for the design and structure of activities. By trying to connect to as many intelligences as possible you will create dynamic and engaging activities.

INVOLVEMENT

Whenever you find yourself tempted to 'tell' the audience something, remember it is less likely they will either listen or remember this piece of information. Instead think about how they can be involved in the message you want to give, there are a wide variety of ways you can involve an audience in your presentation.

For references and links from this chapter visit chris-atkinson.co.uk/books

PROPS

Slides, pictures and flipcharts are commonplace and can be easily forgotten. Bringing in a physical prop, exhibit or sample to illustrate your message will make it memorable. Think creatively, the prop can be metaphorical rather than literal!

SHOWMANSHIP

Showmanship is the best way to achieve that desirable word of 'charismatic'. The rewards of effectively delivered showmanship are huge but so are the risks! Make sure you plan, prepare and practise your showmanship idea until you are completely certain of it.

JOKES AND ANECDOTES

Jokes should only be attempted if you are widely considered a funny person. For everyone else the most effective use of humour is through stories and anecdotes of real life things that have happened to you. Anecdotes have many advantages over joke telling and are far more credible.

CHAPTER 4

FACILITATION SKILLS

Facilitation skills are in fact the embodiment of great leadership and coaching. I would find it hard to train a facilitator without, at the same time, developing that person as a coach. Facilitation is leadership in action; it involves motivating, guiding and supporting others in the development of ideas. So far we've focused on presenting information to an audience in order to inform or educate them in a particular subject. Conversely with facilitation, as with coaching, the audience is the expert. The role of the facilitator is to use their skills to guide the audience to produce its own answers.

There is one large selling point for learning facilitation skills: you don't need to memorise anything, you don't need to be the centre of attention, you don't need slides, and you don't need to be an expert or claim expertise in a subject. Essentially, as a facilitator, your job is to get the audience to consider, discuss and reflect on the points in the agenda. Ideally you are guiding rather than leading the conversation, to ensure maximum value is being extracted from the potential in the room. For this reason, people who struggle with showmanship, joke telling and being the centre of attention find their natural strength in facilitation.

Extroverts who thrive on being the centre of attention can also benefit from strengthening their facilitation skills. Where they may be accused of showboating, facilitating allows them to step away from the spotlight and direct it at their audience, increasing their audience engagement and, consequently, their credibility.

Good facilitation rapidly creates engagement because the audience feels it is driving the conversation, and a powerful facilitator can potentially achieve even higher levels of engagement and participation than the charismatic extrovert who uses lots of high energy showmanship.

The role of the facilitator is quite different to that of the traditional meeting leader, and this difference often catches managers out. A manager might claim to 'facilitate' a meeting but they may, in reality, do little by way of true facilitation. The table below highlights the differences between the roles of facilitator and leader:

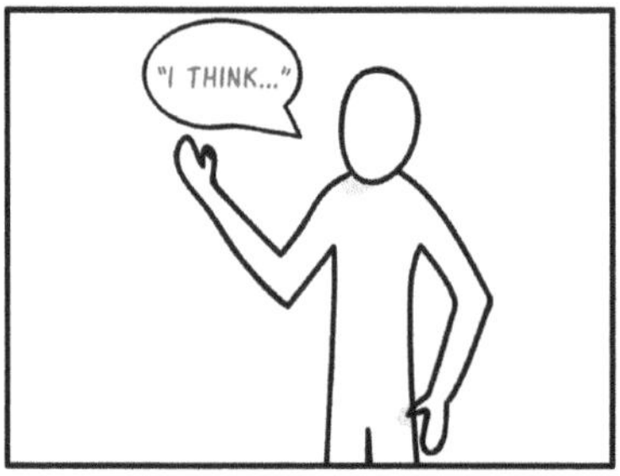

MEETING LEADER

FACILITATOR

Focus on their own needs or departmental objectives and see the group as supporting them	Focus on the needs and objectives of the group and see their role as supporting the group
Concentrate on the content of the discussion	Concentrate on the process of the session to maximise the effectiveness of everyone's contribution
Believe that they are the experts and know best, therefore do a lot of telling	Believe that the group members are the experts and therefore do a lot of listening
Ask few questions and any questions asked are typically closed or leading questions, seeking specific factual information leading the group to a particular answer	Use open and probing questions to explore issues transparently
Strive to put forward their own ideas and work towards a solution they would want	Coach and support the group to develop ideas and solutions which are best supported by the group, as well as being practical for the organisation

A skilled facilitator will make the process look effortless. When you watch a great facilitator, essentially you will see someone doing little more than asking questions. For this reason, many people think facilitation is a great excuse to avoid formal presentations - no preparation needed, no scripting of a presentation, you just turn up and ask some questions! Sounds great! Although there is an element of truth to that, mastering the art of facilitation takes a lot of practice, a great deal of skill and certainly does require preparation. Let's look at the role of facilitator in more detail.

The first rule in facilitation is that **you must remain neutral.** Your personal feelings should be put to one side so that you become a vehicle for the group to explore their feelings on the subject. If you allow your feelings on the matter to surface, it will influence the direction of your questioning and could put off individuals from voicing their true opinions. In other words, if the audience suspects you have a view on a subject, it will affect how they then speak about that subject. It can be very challenging for managers with lots of expertise and experience to remain in this neutral stance. Their background knowledge will constantly tempt them to form an opinion or lead the discussion in a certain direction.

Secondly, the facilitator **must not feel a responsibility for fixing the problem** or finding a solution. The moment you feel a sense of responsibility you stop being neutral as a facilitator and become directive. The facilitator must assume the answers lie within the audience and therefore the audience must work through the issues to reach a conclusion. If the group is struggling, it is the facilitator's job is to keep the conversation constructive and focused, not to rescue them. The facilitator should not feel guilty if the group fails to reach a conclusion; as long as the discussion was facilitated properly the outcome or the success of the session is the group's responsibility.

Here are some initial behavioural guidelines for great facilitation:

- Be assertive, not aggressive or defensive
- Reflect any questions or comments back to the group
- Ask other people's opinions to get a broad range of views
- Treat everyone equally

There are two important skills that are vital for great facilitation - **listening** and **questioning**. Mastery of these two skills is not as easy as you imagine! Let's look at each in more detail.

4.1 Listening skills

Much has been written about the art of listening, and there are many resources available on this subject, but from experience I know people tend to gloss over sections on listening because they assume there is little to learn about such a straightforward subject. If the subject intrigues you, there are lots of additional tips and resources available online which can be found by searching for 'active listening'.

The most important point about developing your listening skills is that, far from being a very natural skill, you have to make a conscious and deliberate effort to listen. Yes, of course you hear naturally, but hearing isn't the same as *listening*. You hear things naturally in a passive way, letting the sound fall onto your ears. The process of listening requires much more effort, which is why most people refer to the skill as 'active listening'. When facilitating, it is important you never assume you are listening; you must always be focused on really listening to:

- What is being said (language used)
- How it is being said (mood, attitude, emotions)
- What is not being said (hesitancies, omissions, inconsistencies)

If you accept that listening is a skill, then you must also accept that it is something you can practise and that by practising you will improve. For that reason you must dedicate yourself to practising and developing your ability to listen.

Many people I work with are offended when I tell them this.

The idea that they are not already accomplished in what they perceive to be such a simple thing can feel patronising, but it mustn't. The more effort and focus you put into your listening the better you will get; the better your listening the better you will be as a facilitator (or as coach, leader, salesperson, consultant and many other roles that require excellent listening skills).

You are not listening to me when...

- You say you understand me before you really know me or my situation
- You have an answer to my problem before I've finished telling you what my problem is
- You cut me off before I've finished speaking
- You finish my sentence
- You find me boring
- You are impatient to tell me something
- You tell me about your own experiences making mine seem unimportant
- You follow your own thoughts and memories when they are triggered by my words

4.2 Advanced open and closed questions

There are more bad habits associated with questioning than with any other skill and technique discussed in this book. No matter how effective you believe you are at asking questions, it's very likely you would be horrified to discover how your performance rates against the standards required for great facilitation. A simple way to evaluate this is to ask a colleague or audience member to write down every question you ask, ensuring they:

i) Write *every* question you ask no matter how small

ii) Write down the question word for word.

This is so important because the nature of your questions will determine the response you get. Your questions are your main tools for facilitation; they establish the rapport between you and the group and maintain the flow of the conversation. You need to design each question so that it achieves the maximum return from the audience. As a facilitator, you should shape and craft a question as an artist creates a piece of art. Unlike an artist, however, you don't have the luxury of time and so this skill needs to become automatic.

You are probably familiar with the idea of open and closed questions. Closed question can be answered with a one-word answer (often yes or no) whereas open questions illicit a fuller, more detailed response. Unsurprisingly, a facilitator will tend to use open questions because the fuller the answer the more information there is to work with. Closed questions can be useful for quickly establishing facts or for narrowing down a discussion, but generally speaking they are of limited value.

The biggest challenge here is that people are unaware how many of their questions are, in fact, closed questions. Any questions starting with 'did', 'does', 'have', 'has', 'are', 'is' or 'can' are invariably closed questions. As we know, these questions require short answers and discourage any discussion, but there is a far greater problem with closed questions which is largely overlooked. Let's imagine you are about to ask:

"So is that because…?"

"Have you tried…?"

"Can you go to…?"

Where do the words needed to complete those questions come from? When we use closed question we are in fact inserting our own suggestions, opinions, beliefs, assumptions or experiences. But, as we discussed at the beginning of this chapter, the facilitator must remain neutral. The moment you ask this type of question your ability to facilitate is compromised; you are putting yourself into the question and thereby limiting the answers of the audience.

"So is that because you don't have enough time, or enough money?"

Time and money are the assumptions of the facilitator and this narrows the focus of the audience. A far better question would be:

"So why is that?"

If it is time, or money, or something else, they will tell you! You don't need to make the suggestion, nor should you try to impress your audience by making such guesses.

"Have you tried talking to your line manager?"

Essentially means "I suggest you speak with your line manager". You know it and your audience will know it! So once again, we need to keep the questions simple.

"What have you tried?"

The answers you get may surprise you and, more importantly, you haven't influenced the audience. Don't contaminate your questions with your own ideas; when you craft your question keep it clean i.e. keep it free from you! The simplest questions are most often the best.

As we see in the examples above, an easy rule of thumb to turn a closed question into an open one is to put one of the following words at the start of the question, and remove your own suggestions.

What	**Which**	**Where**	**CAUTION:** 'Why?' Can sound like an accusation so must be used with a friendly, curious tone
When	**Who**	**How**	

For the best chance of getting full, transparent answers, it is important you learn how to mentally change the closed question into an open one that is 'clean' of your opinion.

There are two methodologies of questioning which can help categorise all these question types that I've mentioned. Interestingly both are often represented as pyramids, with more challenging questions represented higher up the pyramid. The first methodology comes from the field of education and is known as Bloom's Taxonomy[34]. It provides a framework for questioning about the different levels of learning that have taken place. These start with questions around remembering (yes/no), then progress upwards through understanding (which), applying (who, when, where), analysing (what), synthesizing (how) and evaluation (why). The second methodology comes from the world of NLP (Neuro Linguistic Programming[35]) and in particular the work of Robert Dilts who was one of the first to write on the topic of NLP. In his book "**Modeling with NLP**"[36] he creates a structure of questioning that echoes the earlier work in Bloom's Taxonomy. In his approach, we start with questions around surroundings (where, when) then move upwards through behaviour (what), skills (how) and beliefs/values (why).

Both of these methodologies suggest a common hierarchy, with closed questions and factual questions lower in the pyramid. 'What' and 'how' questions are higher up and 'why' questions are at the top, meaning they are the most searching or challenging to answer.

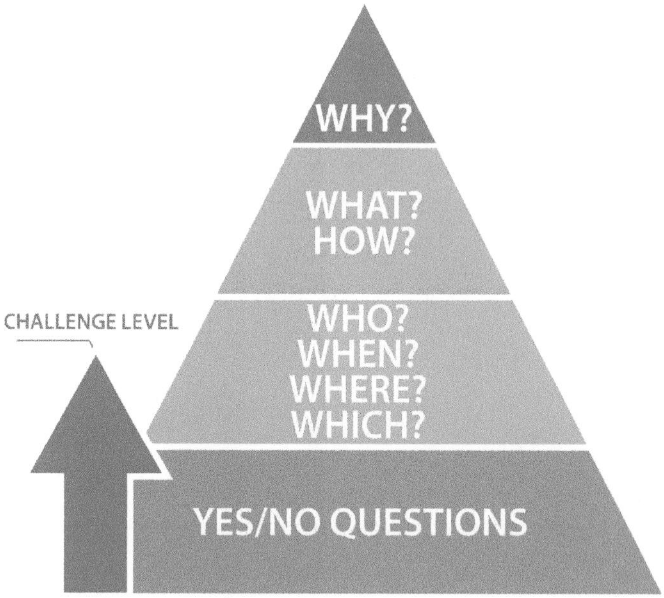

4.3 Floodlight/spotlight and horizontal/vertical questioning techniques

Although changing your questioning habits will be hard work, on its own it won't make you a great facilitator. Once you have mastered how to form good questions you then have to decide how to direct the question to the group and how challenging or searching you want the question to be! [36]

The techniques are summarised below:

Floodlight *questioning is when you ask a question to the entire group.*

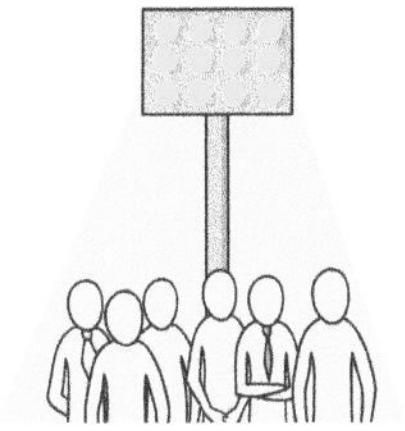

Spotlight *questions target a specific person in the group either because you are interested in finding out more about their thoughts on the subject specifically or because they have been quiet and you are curious about their opinions.*

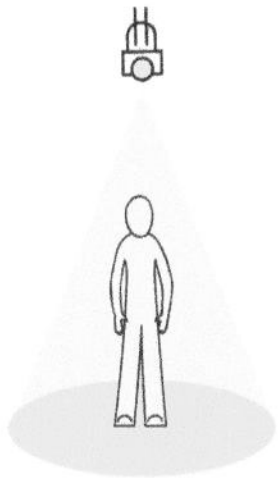

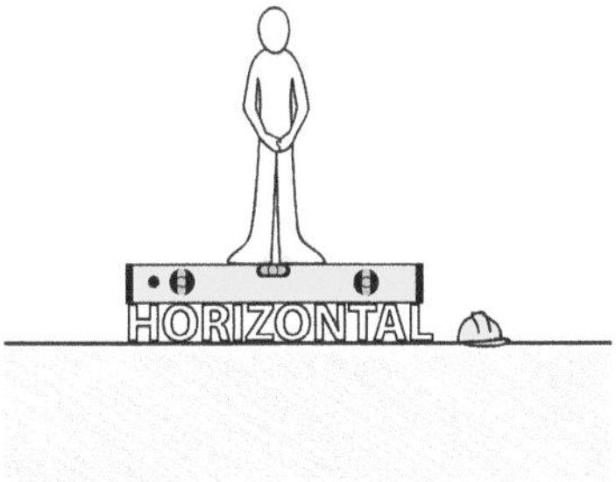

Horizontal *questions are easy to answer and stay at the same level of depth, they do not probe.*

The most common horizontal question is "what else?"

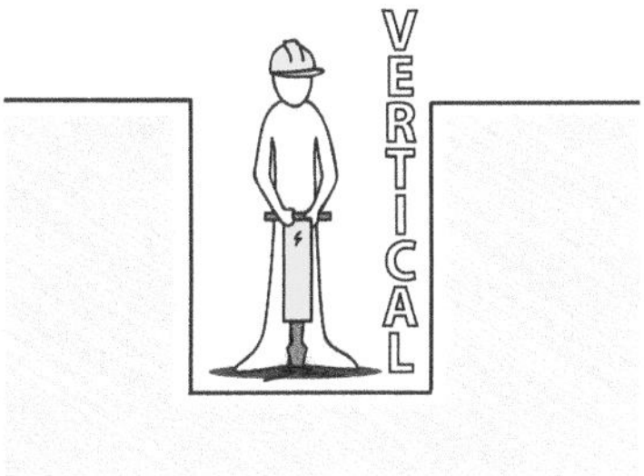

Vertical *questions are probing, they dig deeper into the issue exploring causes, attitudes, beliefs and hidden factors. What, how and why are the most common examples of vertical questions (although please refer to the caution over the use of 'why' in the previous section).*

The tactics can be combined in different ways depending on the needs of the audience to create flow, momentum, focus or debate. Skilled facilitators move effortlessly between the four techniques to create a dynamic and engaging conversation with the audience.

We imagined two scenarios earlier in section 3.3. These looked at ways to involve an audience in a conversation using engagement activities based on multiple intelligences. Now let's imagine running those scenarios again as pure facilitation. Here is an example of a possible question flow (you will have to imagine the audience responses).

Scenario 1: Running a team meeting to create a plan for the upcoming 12 months

Imagine we meet again 12 months from today, what would you like to be different? **Floodlight/Horizontal**

What else? **Floodlight/Horizontal**

Sam, tell me more about what you mean by better teamwork? **Spotlight/Vertical**

How do you all feel that change Sam is suggesting would impact us? **Floodlight/Vertical**

Ravi, this idea would affect your department significantly, what do you think? **Spotlight/Horizontal**

What other ideas do you all have for where we want to be 12 months today? **Floodlight/Horizontal**

John, you have been rather quiet, what are your thoughts? **Spotlight/Horizontal**

Why is that so important to you John? **Spotlight/Vertical**

So we have heard a lot of ideas and a lot of variety, which ideas feel like they are the most important for us to focus on and prioritise? **Floodlight/Vertical**

Scenario 2: Release of new government regulation affecting your industry

How do you feel about government regulation? **Floodlight/Horizontal**

In what ways has regulation impacted you in the past? **Floodlight/Vertical**

Kim, that's a strong opinion, what do you feel could have been done differently? **Spotlight/Vertical**

What do you already know about the upcoming regulation changes? **Floodlight/Horizontal**

What concerns do you have about the possible impact of these latest changes? **Floodlight/Vertical**

Pat, what are your thoughts? **Spotlight/Horizontal**

Who else agrees with Pat? **Floodlight/Horizontal**

We've discussed a lot of things so far, what questions do you have? **Floodlight/Horizontal**

Initially it can be difficult to distinguish between a horizontal and a vertical question. An easy way to tell them apart is through the response of the individual or group answering the question. A vertical question requires a pause for thought before answering; if there is no pause it is likely to be a horizontal question which hasn't probed the issue too deeply. A really good vertical question can stop an individual or group in their tracks, and it is in that moment of deeper thought that you are really adding value as a facilitator.

Sometimes you will want to stay on the surface to generate momentum and pace (horizontal), and other times you will become a challenging coach by probing and digging deeper into the issues (vertical). Sometimes you will want the input of the whole group (floodlight) and at others you will focus on specific people to explore their ideas and thoughts (spotlight). In order to facilitate effectively, you must master the art of combining these techniques so there is a continuous flow. Eventually you will be like the conductor of an orchestra who is in control of the pace and intensity of the music being played.

4.4 Context vs relevance

Context and relevance are largely assumed to be very similar, if not the same, but this couldn't be further from the truth. Understanding the distinction between these two things will make you a much better facilitator. Let us first consider the meaning of 'relevance'. When a speaker is trying to make the subject relevant to the audience we can see the two things as separate:

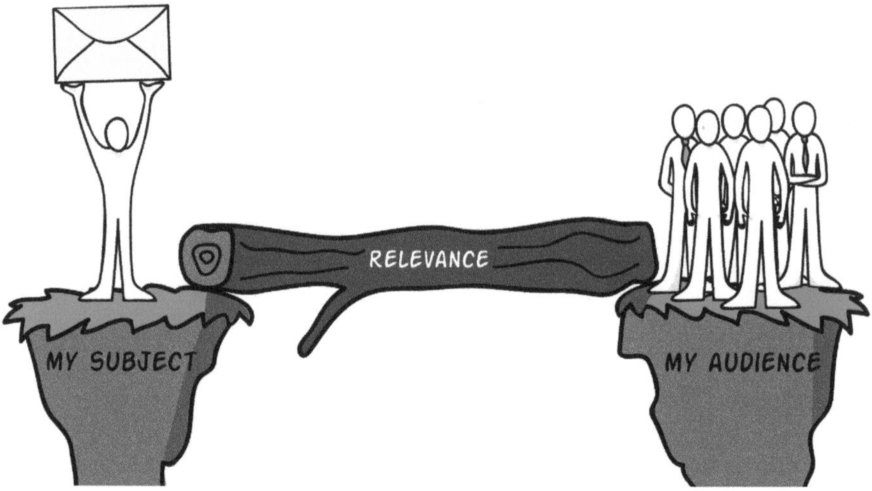

The speaker must connect the topic to the audience and demonstrate how it is relevant to their situation. This is normally done by explaining what it is, why it matters, how it will work and so on. Most presenters and leaders are quite effective at this step but, because they don't understand the concept of context, they fail to have the impact they expected. If you have ever felt that despite your presentation going well it failed to deliver the result you wanted, or, if you were ever surprised when you encountered hostility, then you probably missed 'context'.

Context is actually far more important to establish than relevance, but for many this seems counterintuitive. Context is the missing element for many meetings, training sessions and facilitations that I have seen over my career. By mastering this step you will uncover a wealth of information which will be vital to gaining commitment later in the process, moreover the audience will often engage far quicker and more passionately with context than they will with a conversation about relevance. You will be amazed what comes out when you open up this conversation!

Context is what is wrapped around the entire situation; with strong enough context the relevance becomes self-evident to your audience. Context is all of the background to the topic and includes **circumstances, history**, **attitudes** and **culture** amongst other things.

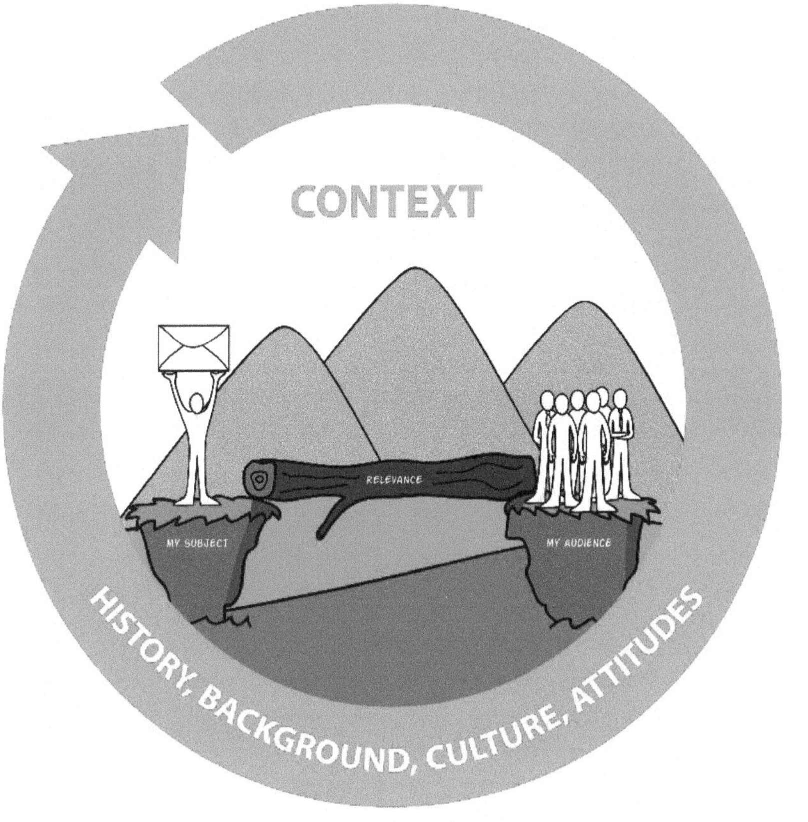

A strong facilitator must invest time, patience and care in exploring the context with the audience. The longer you spend on this stage, the easier the rest of the facilitation will be because you will have established a greater transparency and understanding about the true situation. If you bypass the context, you will spend most of your time trying to persuade the audience about the topic's relevance.

Weaker facilitators are tempted into the more immediately satisfying path of focusing on relevance. Emotionally this route will feel more like addressing the topic in hand which creates a feeling of progress. Unfortunately, this leads to surface level facilitation and by failing to explore the deeper roots of context, the facilitator misses vital conversations.

Let's consider our two scenarios again:

Scenario 1: Running a team meeting to create a plan for the upcoming 12 months

As the facilitator you focus on explaining how important it is for the team to have a direction for the future, and you emphasise the value of creating a clear strategy to achieve this vision. This, however is all relevance; by not exploring the context of the session you have missed that:

When a similar session was held last year all their input was ignored by the previous manager. This manager went ahead implementing their own ideas so now in your session the group will play along politely with your request but will not give their true thoughts and do not believe it will matter

There is a rumour circulating of a restructure or takeover which you know nothing about and so the team feel the entire session is pointless

The team don't respect or trust you as their leader

Hopefully not all three of the above! But you can see that without exploring context, no matter how hard you emphasise the relevance of a 12 month plan it won't matter because context trumps relevance.

DON'T
MISS THE
CONTEXT!

Scenario 2: Release of new government regulation affecting your industry

As the facilitator you focus on explaining how important it is for the team to understand the new regulations. You emphasise the risks in terms of liability if the organisation gets it wrong. Again, this is all relevance, by not exploring the context of the session you have missed that:

Another, rather aggressive, senior manager has asked the team to ignore certain regulations because the department is behind on budgets. The team are scared to reveal this and feel conflicted about what is right

There is long running internal joke (that you are not aware of) about regulatory changes, calling them irrelevant because they are constantly changing and are never audited

This is the tenth regulatory update that the team has had in the last 6 months and they are all totally fed up

All of these background, cultural or attitudinal factors will massively influence the reaction of the audience to the topic. The example of an aggressive manager is also not an exaggeration - I have encountered many teams who are afraid to speak about inappropriate requests from a senior manager. Even though they know it's not right, concern for their careers keeps them quiet.

To summarise, when structuring your questions it is vital that they first explore the context of the subject. You must build a full and clear picture of the attitudes, culture, history and beliefs of the group towards the topic. Once you have this information, the positioning of your subject will be far more powerful. If you have successfully facilitated this conversation about context, you won't have to fight to create the relevance; it becomes a natural outcome of the context.

4.5 Critical components of fantastic facilitation

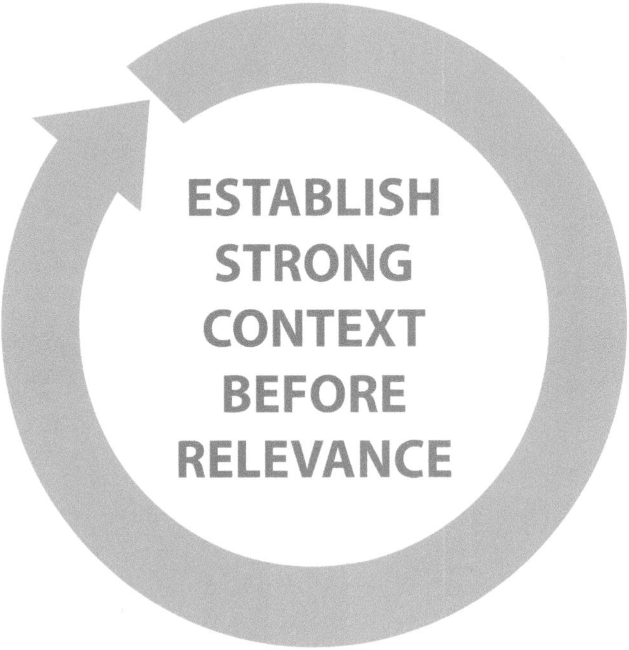

REMEMBER

- The facilitator does not have the answer
- A facilitator is a leader, a builder of people
- People will support what they feel they are part of
- Keep the balance 80/20, 80% Listening, 20% Questioning
- Answers are inside people, the facilitator helps to bring them out
- Facilitation is a dynamic, spontaneous, growing, energising process

CHAPTER SUMMARY

LISTENING

This is not as natural a skill as you imagine. Good listening takes significant effort, as does the ability to clearly demonstrate to others that you are listening!

QUESTIONING

Open and closed questions are more complex than simply the difference between yes/no questions and who, what, when, where, which, how and why. It is important that you develop and sharpen your questioning technique to ensure you are asking questions that provoke a detailed answer.

FLOODLIGHT SPOTLIGHT

Use floodlight to involve the whole group and spotlight to target specific audience members who you might want to hear from.

For references and links from this chapter visit chris-atkinson.co.uk/books

HORIZONTAL VERTICAL

Use horizontal questioning techniques to build engagement and momentum with the group. Use vertical questions to provoke deeper thinking and challenge the group.

CONTEXT VS RELEVANCE

Context beats relevance! Most professionals understand the importance of explaining the subject's relevance to the audience but most fail to establish or uncover the context. Start by establishing clear context with the group, this ensures you address the true issues and the relevance will follow naturally.

4

CHAPTER

5

INSPIRING OTHERS

If you do an internet search for "inspiration" you will find quite literally millions of results - most commonly pictures, quotations and stories. But all of those things are designed to inspire you; none of them address the critical question of how to become inspirational. I think there's a huge gap in the market here.

Authors Kouzes and Posner[37] asked a group of people to say the first thing that came to mind when they heard the words 'Paris, France'. Not one mentioned the size, economic situation or the population. They all spoke about the images they see in their minds' eye: the Eiffel Tower, the Arc de Triomphe, romance, great food and so on. Similarly, in our communication we need to use words and images that evoke sights, sounds, tastes, smells, and feelings. *"People aren't persuaded by the facts as much as they are by the emotions, feelings, and images behind those facts,"* say Kouzes and Posner.

This chapter is your 'how to' guide to move away from the dry facts and figures of organisational communication and to become a more inspirational speaker. We will explore what inspiration is, what you need to demonstrate as a speaker and the three key strategies used to become more inspiring.

5.1 What is inspiration and why is it so important?

To find out what makes a bad boss, researchers Zenger and Folkman[38] analysed the behaviour of 30,000 managers, using information from 300,000 of their peers. Out of this group of 30,000 they firstly focused on the 11,000 leaders who received the lowest scores on their 360 feedback reports — the bottom 1% and the bottom 10%. Then they analysed a group of executives whose employment had recently been terminated, similarly combing through the data looking for clues to explain why they had failed.

By combining conclusions from these two groups, they were able to identify 10 fatal flaws that contribute to a leader's failure. None of these flaws appeared in the feedback for the contrasting group of 'effective leaders'. They found that bosses are defined as 'bad' because of certain critical things they don't do, rather than the appalling things they do.

*Number 1 on their list of 10 fatal flaws was **FAILURE TO INSPIRE** because of a lack of energy and enthusiasm.*

Failed leaders were repeatedly described by their colleagues as unenthusiastic and passive in their communication. This was, in fact, the most noticeable of all their failings and this is the main focus of this chapter. Inspiration is often spoken about in business and speakers are frequently told to "go and inspire them", but it is quite shocking how little people really know about what inspiration is, what it means and, most importantly, how to achieve it!

Firstly, some key questions:

When you experience inspiration, where do you physically feel it?

Most people say it is felt more in their chest/heart than in their head. Simply put this means 'inspiration' is a feeling or an emotion. So, inspiring people is more an emotional experience than an intellectual experience.

Why is that important?

Because we can conclude that if you want to inspire people you must aim to generate a positive emotional response in those people.

What is the leader's role in this?

Here is an interesting point. Based on the previous questions we have to conclude that you can't force people to be inspired! Inspiration is a feeling in the other person; all you can do is create the right environment for the other person to experience that emotion, then wait. The best way to elicit an emotional response in other people is by showing emotions yourself. It is hard to imagine a cold, unemotional speaker arousing a powerful emotional response except perhaps anger or frustration! We will come to these in a moment. Only by displaying emotion yourself can you expect an emotional response in others.

How often do you see other people showing strong clear positive emotions in your organisation?

This sits at the heart of the issue and it is quite a significant problem within our organisations. Many organisational cultures place so much importance on targets, intellectual arguments, performance and practical matters that emotions - particularly positive ones - don't really have a place. When I encourage a client to show their passion or talk from a more emotional position they are usually embarrassed and extremely hesitant about communicating in that way in front of colleagues.

Think about what emotions are acceptable or commonplace in your organisation. Most likely you are thinking of anger or frustration. These seem to be the acceptable professional emotions. An angry boss hitting the table or shouting at a team is not so unusual, and is regularly tolerated by organisations and team members. How often do you hear about, or experience, a boss speaking with heartfelt passion in a way that inspires you? We rarely witness emotions and are embarrassed about showing our emotions; the emotions we do occasionally see are negative and rarely challenged. What does this say about the culture of our organisations? This is certainly not an effective route to engagement or inspiration! Here's the first step to being more inspirational:

5.2 Showing authenticity

> “*Authenticity is a collection of choices that we have to make every day. It's about the choice to show up and be real. The choice to be honest. The choice to let our true selves be seen.* **Dr Brené Brown**

How inspirational we are as a speaker is largely down to authenticity. As articulated so wonderfully by Dr Brené Brown, it is about how genuine you are when you speak and how much comes from the heart. The more authentic you are the more likely you are to inspire others. This is the good news: to be more inspirational you actually have to *do* less.

This might sound easy, but researchers have recognised the huge challenges leaders face when trying to become more authentic. Many leaders try to act a certain way at work, with their 'true' personality only emerging outside of work in personal situations and relationships. For most, this professional mask has become such a normal part of their role that they are no longer aware of it, nor do they realise how much emotional effort is committed to maintaining it.

We pay a heavy price for this dichotomy of personality. In his article ***Leaders, Drop Your Masks,*** published in Harvard Business Review, Peter Fuda writes:

> *"There are two main ways in which leaders wear masks. Some conceal their perceived inadequacies behind the polished facade we have come to expect of "great" leaders, a bit like the Phantom from Andrew Lloyd Webber's epic musical The Phantom of the Opera. Others take on a new persona at work that they feel is necessary for success, much like Jim Carrey's character Stanley Ipkiss in the movie The Mask, who transforms into a flamboyant green superhero. Both types of mask undermine trust and effectiveness. They also create inner conflict, as leaders struggle to align their work and private lives."*[39]

It's widely recognised that we are experiencing a crisis of trust in society. Scandals, excesses of greed and shocking revelations have destroyed much of our trust in politicians, leaders and figures of authority. The increasing importance of authenticity is a clear response to this situation, even to the extent that it has become the subject of high level journalism and research. Rob Goffee and Gareth Jones discuss this in ***Managing Authenticity: The Paradox of Great Leadership:***[40]

> *"It is also a response to the public's widespread disenchantment with politicians and business people. We all suspect that we're being duped ... Our growing dissatisfaction with sleek, airbrushed leadership is what makes authenticity such a desirable quality in today's corporations — a quality that, unfortunately, is in short supply."*

Goffee and Jones have published some of the most powerful and clearly articulated work on leadership and I emphatically encourage you to read their articles and papers. Authenticity is directly related to trust: when we are authentic people trust us. When people trust us they listen openly and without suspicion or filters. Once your audience is willing to receive your communication in this way, all you need to do is speak from the heart with clear emotional content and your feelings will be transmitted. This is the process that sits behind inspiration.

When I first started working internationally, much of my work was with petrochemical clients from the Gulf states. Almost exclusively these clients were Arab men and because at the time I was quite young, these men were all significantly older than me. On one of my early programmes I cheerily introduced myself to a participant, the person paused, looked me up and down, then asked "are there any *other* speakers?" When I answered that it was just me, he asked a series of challenging questions about my age and qualifications to do this role. This incident was followed by a series of similar comments on other programmes with the same client where my age was questioned. Having been very successful within the UK for many years without any incidents like this it completely shook my confidence. It caused a great deal of soul searching about whether I was ready for this level of international work. With my confidence shaken I started thinking of ways to appear more mature in the eyes of participants. One day I decided to experiment, although I was unmarried at the time I tried wearing a ring on my wedding finger. Whether the resulting change was real or only in my mind I will never know but instantly something was different, my clients stopped asking about my age, they seemed to listen more and be more willing to engage with what I was saying. As I look back to that time I realise the 'married man' was a mask I was wearing to protect myself from the feeling of insecurity I had about my age when working with a senior audience from the Gulf states. The mask seemed harmless at the time but there is no doubt in my mind that, to some extent, I was putting on an act rather than being my authentic self.

The first step to becoming an inspirational leader or communicator is to remove the masks you are wearing. This process can be uncomfortable and can make you feel vulnerable, but it can be done in stages. You can slowly become more authentic each time you speak, using the techniques in the following chapters to reveal things about yourself or show feelings more transparently.

Dr Brené Brown's famous TED talk about vulnerability[41] highlights the importance and benefits of showing this side of your character:

> *Vulnerability sounds like truth and feels like courage. Truth and courage aren't always comfortable, but they're never weakness.*
> **Dr Brené Brown**

I understand why leaders and speakers feel they must be perfect, that they must display strength and confidence. To an extent this is true; we should look confident and secure when presenting. But which speaker will look stronger and more confident to you: the one who puts on a mask, who pretends they know everything and feels a little 'fake' to the audience, or the speaker who shows that they don't know everything, that there are some things that concern them and that they need their colleagues in order to succeed? We want our business leaders to be authentic, and we've learned that this authenticity and genuine confidence is demonstrated through vulnerability, passion and truthful feelings.

As you learn to trust yourself and your audience you will feel less compelled to maintain your mask. Speaking will quickly feel easier and you will feel lighter and less burdened. This is not a small thing. To your audience this could be the single most important thing you do.

A NOTE OF CAUTION

Being open, genuine and authentic does not mean you have to reveal your darkest thoughts or issues. Going into a business meeting and baring your soul is likely to be inappropriate in many organisational contexts. Inevitably there will be things which are not appropriate to be shared in the work environment. Based on your relationship with your team or the organisational culture, only you will know where those boundaries lie. You should be aware that oversharing can also drive some people away.

Authenticity is about letting people see the person you are. The fact that you're not perfect, that you have challenges and are vulnerable, inspires others to follow you and, paradoxically, makes you look stronger.

5.3 The three routes to inspiration

During the research for this book I talked to a lot of people about their experiences of inspiration. I asked participants on each training course and seminar I delivered to describe the experience of feeling inspired or a person who inspires them. From their stories, I concluded the casual factors for inspiration fell broadly into three categories. Two of these categories were unsurprising, but I had not expected the third one and its discovery felt rather uncomfortable. We will discuss that later in the chapter!

Here is what I discovered:

1. Empathy
2. Desire
3. Fear

Empathy: This expands on our discussion about authenticity. When you show genuine emotion in your speech the audience will start imagining and relating to how you are feeling. They will quickly feel involved in the journey you describe. Remember the connection between inspiration and emotion - if people feel emotions from your communication then they are rapidly on the road to inspiration. Storytelling is a fast and effective way of encouraging inspiration.

Desire: Sounds good doesn't it? Desire is the powerful feeling of wanting something to happen or wanting ownership of something. But creating desire is not as easy as it sounds and the audience may be attracted to very different things to you. Additionally, the abstract corporate language used in organisations often prevents a strong emotional connection to the topic. Using imagery and pictures is a quick and simple way to connect the logical mind to the emotional mind, which can help create desire. Used in conjunction with props and exhibits this will dramatically affect your audience.

Fear: This one was a surprise to me. I considered omitting it from this book because of the negative connotations and experiences connected with it. Many people described being 'inspired' to change by a sudden and cold realisation about something that terrified them. Commonly this was a health scare or an unfortunate incident involving someone close to them. Fear quickly generates emotions that may cause us to act a certain way or change our behaviour, but is this still inspiration? I'll let you decide later in this chapter!

Whichever route you choose, you must learn to use all of the senses to create a vivid picture so the experience is immersive for your audience. Once the audience's emotions are engaged through your descriptions, inspiration will follow.

Summary: Three routes to inspiration

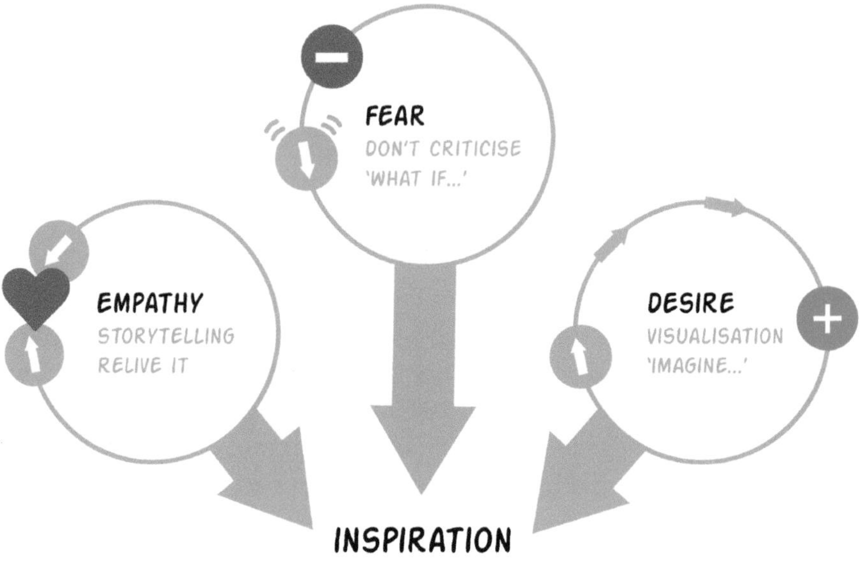

> *We have quite a US-centric view of what inspirational or motivational speakers are like. But the big, on-stage, extroverted characters are just a small subset of inspirational communicators. When you look genuinely at what inspires people, you find that true inspiration is not a result of how extroverted you are, or how over-the-top, or even how impressive you can be. It's about how authentic you are. To what extent you are able to speak from the heart. That's something people overlook when they think about whether they can be inspirational.*
> **Chris Atkinson, featured in Switched on Leadership Magazine**

5.4 Storytelling and empathy

The ability to engage an audience simply through speaking is the greatest skill of a presenter. A good story, a dramatic tale or a funny anecdote can be a powerful tool and will engage your audience from the start. Storytelling is a fundamental skill of leadership and it has been a rich and vital method of communication in human society through the ages. We only have to look at any religious text or cave painting to see that we are storytellers by nature. We learn through stories; they allow complex ideas like morality to be simply communicated. In chapter 3.6 I discussed how anecdotes allow you to connect authentically and intimately with your audience, but they can also help you to inspire others. Anecdotes and stories can have much more depth than people realise.

The research into public speaking and presentations shows overwhelmingly that audiences are more engaged and attentive when listening to stories as opposed to normal speech. Storytelling as an art form has been popularised in recent years, with many courses now available through major universities and business schools. What was once seen as a bit 'soft', or even the domain of the spiritual, has become a solid business subject. In his book ***Leading Minds: An Anatomy of Leadership,***[42] the great Howard Gardner writes that the key to leadership "is the effective communication of a story." This is no small claim. Gardner believes that leaders are individuals who can tell convincing stories and who embody the themes of those stories in their actions. He notes that leaders must also be sensitive to the stories that their audiences already believe and, when necessary, challenge those entrenched narratives.

> “ *It is important for leaders to know their stories; to get them straight; to communicate them effectively, particularly to those who are in the thrall of rival stories; and, above all, to embody in their lives the stories that they tell.* **Howard Gardner**

In his book ***Wired to Care***[43] Dev Patnaik argues that a major flaw in business practice is a lack of empathy within organisations. He claims that the real commercial opportunity for companies is to foster a widely held sense of empathy in their people. Empathic organisations see new opportunities more quickly than competitors, adapt to change more easily, and create workplaces that offer employees a greater sense of purpose in their jobs.

Extract from ***Wired to Care***

> *"Creating that sort of empathic connection to other people can have profound effects on a company, beyond increasing its growth rate. In many cases, it can give new meaning to the work that people do. And often in today's world, it's that sense of meaning that we lack most of all.*
>
> *Most companies can offer competitive salaries, vacation packages, health insurance and retirement plans. But too few of them can demonstrate any sort of connection between the work that we do every day and a positive impact on the wider world. Beyond mere survival and provision for our families, many of us don't have a good reason to go to work in the morning.*
>
> *In addition to its economic impacts, increasing empathy helps you see how much your job makes a difference. And that's the greatest reward of all."*

Sounds a lot like being inspired doesn't it? It should, because this is what is possible when we connect empathically with people. A sense of emotional connection to another person builds a quick and powerful pathway to inspiration.

Here are some additional benefits of stories in presentations:

Benefit to Presenter	Benefit to Audience
Memory - If you use a story you won't have to write notes. To tell a story you just have to remember and relive your experience. This can significantly reduce the stress levels for the presenter. **Emotions** – Normal organisational content can make it hard for presenters to speak emotionally. Stories are rich with feelings and emotions and so are easier for the presenter to deliver with feeling.	**Memorable** – Stories are easily absorbed and recalled by audiences. If well told, a story can be remembered months or even years later. Compare this to your memory of the last corporate presentation you heard! **Simplified** – through analogies or metaphors, stories can simplify complex ideas. A story can be a lot easier for an audience to relate to and understand.

As communicators, our job is to communicate using stories as analogies of everyday business. Your mind may go blank when you try to think of a story, but you experience events every day that could make a great story. Your life is filled with fantastic stories! The key is to recognise how a story can be used as an analogy to illustrate your key points.

Remember: The story is just the vehicle for the message. The message you want to communicate is the only reason you are telling the story. It is essential that you are clear about the message you want to communicate. Once you know your message, you can then think of experiences in your life that will illustrate that message to make a story. It's important to tell the story first, and then use a 'bridge' to link the story with the message it conveys. A phrase like "in the same way..." can be useful to bridge from your personal story to the message. Plan your message carefully and ensure your story bridges clearly to the purpose.

> " *Empathy is what happens to us when we leave our own bodies...and find ourselves either momentarily or for a longer period of time in the mind of the other. We observe reality through their eyes, feel their emotions.* **Ken Lampert**

Types of story

There are four different types of story that are the most useful for inspiration:

1. *Who I am and what I stand for*
2. *Where I come from*
3. *Where I/we are going*
4. *What I've learnt*

You will notice that all of these are quite personal. If you want to inspire others then you must speak personally and from the heart. Ideally your story should be emotionally meaningful to you; the most inspirational stories take you to the edge of control of your feelings. You don't want to lose control or cry but if you are visibly moved your audience will also be moved. Finding a story with the right emotional level is an art form, and it may take a little experimentation and some honest feedback from a trusted audience member.

Type of story	When to use it
Who I am and what I stand for	To emphasise values, beliefs or points of principle To describe your expectations of team behaviour To build trust and understanding
Where I come from	To 'drop the mask' and show your real self To explain your behaviours (and obsessions!) To build trust and understanding
Where I or we are going	To share your personal aspirations (what you hope for) To discuss your vision and the future of the team/department (what we hope for) To explore possible industry or organisational futures (what might be)
What I've learnt	To warn and caution about possible problems To debrief or discuss mistakes that have happened To explain decisions that have been taken

Storytelling is at the heart of leadership

There are a number of common narrative types which most stories will fit into.

Common story narratives:

- Overcoming a challenge
- Connecting with others
- Metaphor
- Discovering potential
- Humorous
- Tales of failure

Knowing the function of these different narratives will help you select an appropriate story for your situation as well as helping you pitch the correct tone for your delivery. For example, it would be a mistake to tell an 'overcoming a challenge' story in a humorous way because the inspirational impact of such a story comes from expressing the feelings you had during that difficult time. Smiling or laughing would be incongruent with the message you are trying to deliver (see congruence in chapter 2.1). The table on the following pages provides more detail on the narrative types and gives you an idea of when you might want to use each.

A NOTE OF CAUTION:

A great story doesn't have to be about a dramatic or traumatic experience; anything can be interesting if it is well told. The drama and power of the story comes from the way you tell it not from the content itself. Although events with strong emotional content do make for effective stories it is by no means the only requirement. A great storyteller finds a good story in everyday experiences. Don't worry if you have had no drama in your life recently - storytelling is far more about *how* you tell something than *what* you are telling.

Descriptions of narrative types and their functions:

Overcoming challenge	
Description: Stories about facing huge pressures or succeeding 'against the odds'. It is important that you discuss and demonstrate how you felt when facing that particular challenge.	**Function**: They show that it's possible to get through challenging periods and that you have experience of pressure. This is useful when people are facing tough situations and are feeling overwhelmed.

Connecting with others	
Description: Stories focusing on the value and importance of relationships. They might cover ways to develop a strong network, the benefits of deepening your relationships with people, or overcoming difficulties with people we don't like.	**Function**: They emphasise the human component in being successful. We need a strong network or team around us to be effective. Sometimes we need to work with people we find difficult, and this kind of story can be helpful.

Metaphor/Analogy	
Description: Sometimes a story can be a metaphor for a lesson in life; think how Aesop's fable about the tortoise and the hare works. In order to inspire, however, your metaphors should be based on real experiences rather than fables.	**Function**: Metaphors and analogies work best when a subject is less well known to the audience or when the content is complex or technical. By relating the subject to an everyday situation using metaphor or analogy it becomes more accessible for the audience.

Discovering potential

Description: These stories are about challenging our assumptions and discovering a greater depth, knowledge, skill or passion than we had first assumed.

Function: The revelation of potential reminds audiences that there may be more to a situation, process, technology or person than they initially thought. It promotes positive thought and open mindedness.

Humorous

Description: Not all stories have to be dramatic and profound. Many of the most memorable and emotional stories are those that make people laugh. These stories are often about your mistakes, noble failures and embarrassing incidents.

Function: Humour is an important tool for building rapport with an audience. Moreover, it can demonstrate to the audience that you are down to earth, approachable, and humble enough to laugh at yourself.

Tales of failure

Description: These are similar to humorous stories about mistakes, noble failures and embarrassing incidents, but they aren't to be laughed at. To make the distinction clear to the audience you must emphasise how it felt for you at the time and show the emotions you went through.

Function: We are increasingly recognising the importance of open discussion, and even celebration, of failure as a natural part of a healthy organisation. If we want people to be creative, improve processes and innovate then we must accept that failure is sometimes inevitable. This type of narrative could be used to warn or caution, but it is most powerful when it demonstrates that we should not be afraid of failure.

Structure of a great story

There are many great books and articles about how to structure a good story. In my experience the best stories are told in a very natural way, so don't get too analytical about how you structure your story. The danger is that whilst manipulating the narrative may create a better 'arc' to the story, you may lose some of your naturalness when you speak. Professional storytellers can often seem artificial or controlled because they have sacrificed their natural style for mastery of their craft. Your story doesn't need an intricate plot; it's better to keep it simple. We can learn from successful playwrights and writers, who use simple storytelling techniques to find emotion and drama in ordinary, everyday events.

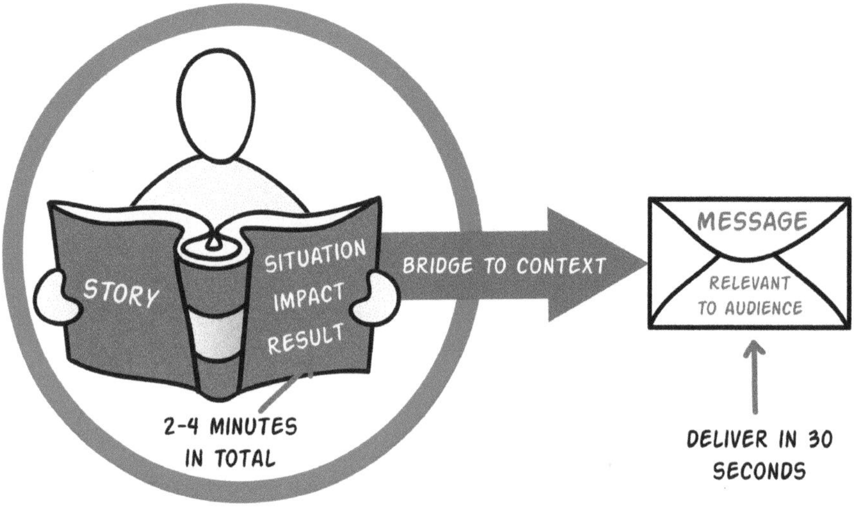

This simple story structure of 'situation - impact - result' will work with any story you use. Having set up the 'situation' briefly, it is important to then connect with the emotions felt at the time as you explain the 'impact' the situation had on you and those around you. Try, as much as possible, to relive the emotions that you experienced at the time. The 'result' (outcome) of your story doesn't need to be happy, or even tidy, but it must be true.

After the result you must bridge (i.e. demonstrate the connection) to the topic of your presentation, showing how and why your story is relevant. Ideally a good story should be 2-4 minutes long, certainly no longer. The message that follows should be short and easy to understand, around 30 seconds maximum in length.

Delivering a great story

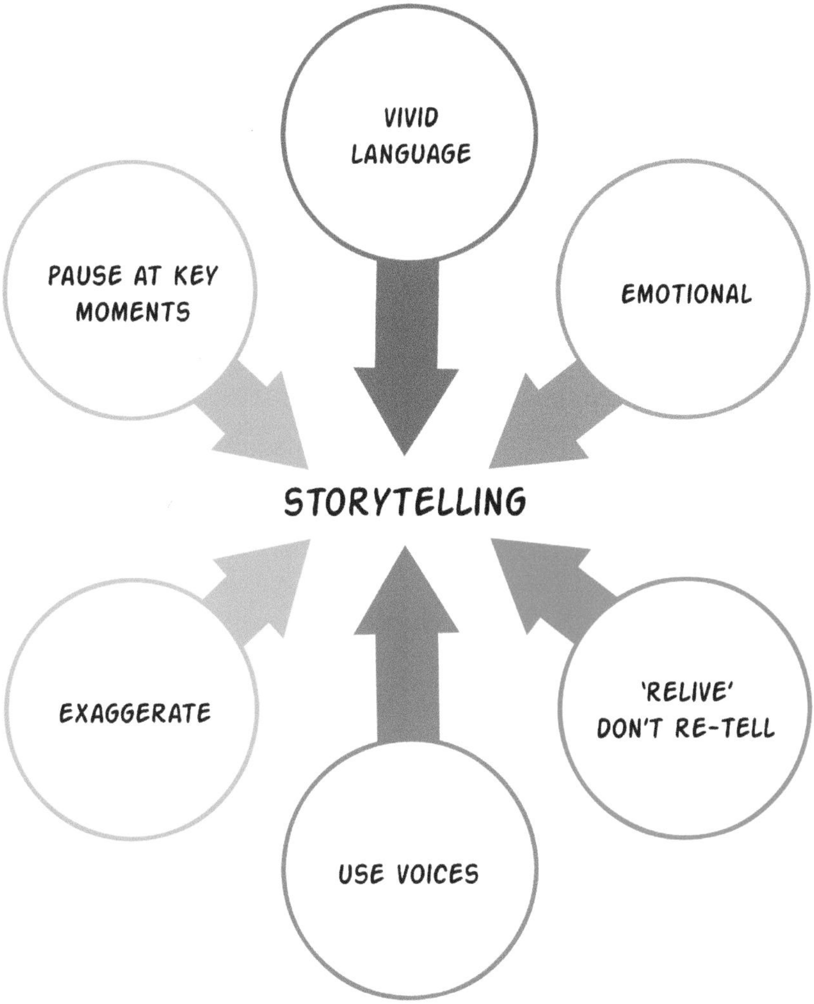

When we tell stories to children it feels natural to give the story drama, to voice different characters or to exaggerate our expressions, but when we tell stories to adults we feel this level of emphasis is patronising or looks foolish. Of course you don't want to address professionals as you would small children, but there is no reason you shouldn't adopt the same principles to make your delivery varied and emphatic. As you develop and practise this skill, you will inevitably feel rather silly and uncomfortable, but this is not how you will appear to your audience. It's important to get feedback from your audience, and to seek out people you trust to give you honest and reliable feedback. Most likely they will tell you that your delivery was strongest when you felt the most 'over the top'.

Vivid language	Use **vivid language** throughout the story. Infuse your story with imaginative, evocative words and eliminate "everyday" vocabulary to avoid telling boring stories. This pulls the audience into your world and sparks their imagination. Don't say "she seemed angry", say "she had fire in her eyes".
Use voices	Speak in the **voice** of the characters. Breathe energy into your stories by giving each character a different voice. Think about the people in your story, the way they speak and move. Whenever a different character is 'speaking', your voice should change to indicate to the audience that this is a different person talking. Use body language to demonstrate the attitudes of each character. ***Note:*** *Be respectful and cautious about mimicking accents; without great care this can appear insensitive.*
Emotional	Don't just tell the facts of the story – speak about the **emotions** you experienced. Talk about why you felt that way. Emotions are always interesting for people, and if you fail to express emotions then you will fail to inspire. If you are concerned about showing too much emotion, then simply say what you were feeling in an energetic way. For example, if in my story I am excited, it would be most effective to physically show this excitement. Alternatively, I could say in an excited voice, "I was so excited!" Saying this in a flat, dull tone would be incongruent and ineffective.

Re-live don't re-tell	Rather than just 'telling' people what happened, the best stories are those that are '**relived**', as if they are being re-enacted. Tell the story in the first person and search your memory for details like the clothes people wore, how they moved, and what things felt like. By reliving the story you will reconnect with the feelings you experienced at that time and you will speak more honestly and emotionally.
Exaggerate	Make **exaggerated** movements and gestures, but don't exaggerate the content of your story. Perform the actions of the characters to illustrate your story as a mime artist might. This entertains the audience and helps them to connect with the plot and characters. It's better to appear overly animated than to appear unenthusiastic. Storytelling is a performance and you need energy and enthusiasm to tell a good story.
Pause at key moments	Allow your audience time to react to the story. **Pause for dramatic effect** to increase interest in your listeners and ensure your story is heard. Avoid rushing through parts of the story because of time pressures - good stories should appear effortless. A proper pause should last for a count to three (as covered in chapter 2.4).

In summary, be passionate about your story, even if it seems silly to do so. Telling a story with a sense of drama raises your energy levels and captivates your audience. Remember to maintain slow, individual eye contact with your audience to demonstrate your confidence and encourage audience members to pay attention. This also helps you to gauge how well your story is being received and allows you to make quick adjustments if necessary. Storytelling is the oldest form of entertainment - it should be dramatic and fun.

5.5 Creating desire through visualisation

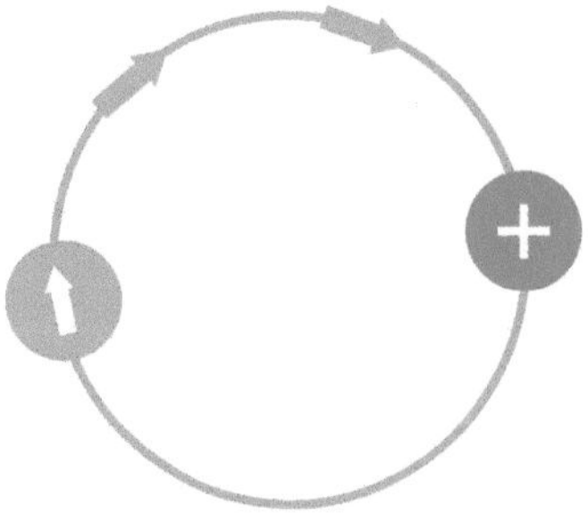

There are two broad types of motivators in life: those that encourage movement towards something and those that encourage movement away from something. You could frame these in the context of pleasure and pain. The 'moving away' motivation moves you away from pain, and the 'moving towards' motivation moves you towards pleasure. This section covers how to create a powerful 'towards' motivation. In chapter 5.6 we will look at 'away from' motivation in the context of fear.

These two motivations are not necessarily connected. If I move away from something that scares me, it does not follow that I'm moving towards something that will give me pleasure. Rather, I am moving back into a neutral state. Both motivations offer a similar outward result, but the different motivations driving the behaviour have profoundly different consequences.

Let's look at these two motivations:

Undirected – the motivation is just to get away; the direction is unimportant

Inconsistent – as we move away and the 'pain' reduces, our motivation decreases

AWAY FROM OR PAIN MOTIVATION

Stressful – driven by fear and discomfort, which can lead to sustained periods of stress

Has a clear focus and target – this helps to get back on-course when you encounter challenges or get diverted

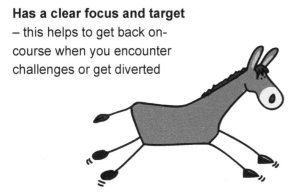

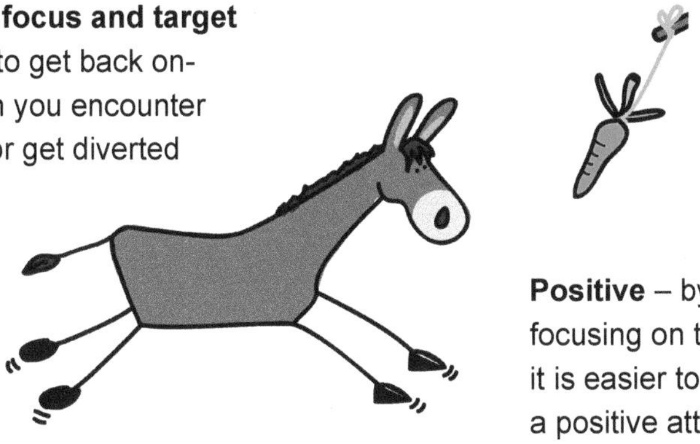

Positive – by focusing on the future it is easier to maintain a positive attitude

TOWARDS OR PLEASURE MOTIVATION

Increasing motivation – the closer you get to your target the greater your enthusiasm and motivation

As leaders and presenters, how do we tap into the power of towards motivation? The towards motivation is strongest when you have a clear mental image of what you want to achieve, and a strong desire to achieve it. A clear vision awakens your inner strength and power, and pushes you forward.

The role of vision

Much has been said and written about the power of a compelling vision. Motivational speakers regularly extol this wisdom, and it is hard to find a book on leadership, self-development or organisational development that does not advocate the importance of creating a vision. An exciting, well-articulated vision generates energy and excitement within a team or organisation. All too often, employees feel that what they are doing has very little meaning or purpose. A vision helps people put meaning into their actions.

A strong vision motivates and energises people, committing them to the project. When people can see that their organisation is committed to a vision, they are more enthusiastic about the direction of that organisation, and more committed to working towards that vision.

> *"Vision should describe a set of ideals and priorities, a picture of the future, a sense of what makes the company special and unique, a core set of principles that the company stands for, and a broad set of compelling criteria that will help define organizational success.*
>
> **Oren Harari**[44]

Sadly, the vision of most organisations across all industries fall very short of Harari's ideals. I'm willing to wager that your organisation's vision - if you a) have one and b) know it - reads something along the lines of:

- To be the number 1 in...
- To be a world leader in...
- To be the best in class at...

How motivational are these statements? To what extent do they inspire and energise your workforce? Do they paint a clear picture of the future and the organisation's direction?

When I encounter a company with one of these visions I encourage the senior leaders to read the vision of their nearest competitor. Their competitor will almost always have a nearly identical vision. How could this be possible? A vision should be a unique commitment. If it is similar to another organisation's then it has definitely missed the mark.

Creating desire through vision at an organisational level is very challenging and only a handful of organisations ever manage to achieve this standard, but this is the subject for another book. If you reduce the size of your target audience it becomes much easier and far more powerful. Using vision to inspire a team or department within an organisation is far more effective than aiming to influence an entire organisation in one go.

Organisations value lasting achievements and excellence, but these are not easy to acquire. Inevitably, in order to obtain these rare results, people must be prepared to face an enormous amount of frustration, difficulty, and disappointment. To encourage them to continue despite these adversities, people need to envision a compelling, magnetic future filled with desirable outcomes. This vision makes people feel they are part of a greater whole, and gives meaning to their work.

Let's look at what makes a great vision...

How to create a powerful vision

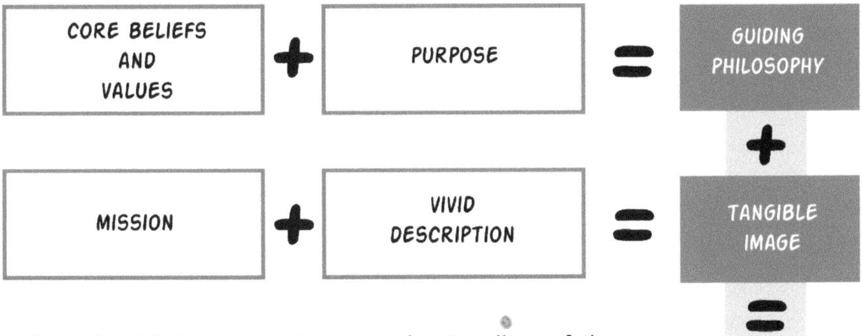

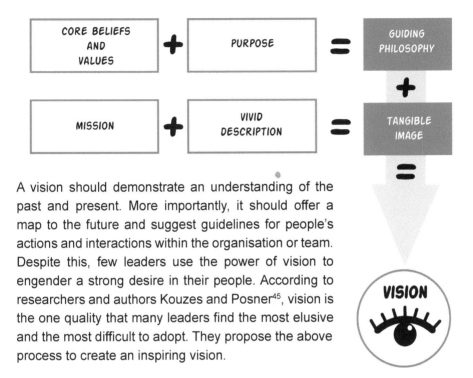

A vision should demonstrate an understanding of the past and present. More importantly, it should offer a map to the future and suggest guidelines for people's actions and interactions within the organisation or team. Despite this, few leaders use the power of vision to engender a strong desire in their people. According to researchers and authors Kouzes and Posner[45], vision is the one quality that many leaders find the most elusive and the most difficult to adopt. They propose the above process to create an inspiring vision.

The first stage of the model illustrates the concept of your **guiding philosophy**. This represents the standards of behaviour and the culture that you aspire to. It is created by expressing your purpose along with the values or beliefs of your organisation. People will only commit to achieving the goal if they have a sense of purpose and direction. A shared sense of purpose is the glue that binds people together, often linking an individual's goals with the organisation's goals. When correctly expressed, a shared sense of purpose overrides individual interests and encourages a co-ordinated, collective effort.

The second major component of the vision model is the **tangible image**. This is composed of the mission and a vivid description. A mission is a declaration of an organisation's core purpose and focus - it's reason for existing. Strong mission statements serve as filters to separate the important from the unimportant and they communicate the intended direction of the organisation.

You may remember we discussed vivid description in the previous section on storytelling. Vision is a type of storytelling based on a potential future. A powerful vision utilises descriptive language, imagery and vivid description.

The most compelling visions are visual, conjuring images in people's minds and painting a picture of how the world *could look*.

When you combine a tangible image with a strong guiding philosophy, you are on the way to a vision that inspires and engages a team or organisation!

Writing a vision – the 3 Ps

Despite all the high quality academic advice there is still a significant shortfall between the visions being created and the aspiration of inspiration and engagement. The following three rules will help you translate a great idea into a truly inspirational vision. These techniques are not commonly heard or used in traditional vision statements so they may feel a little unusual the first time you try them.

Positive Imagery

Many people find it easier to explain what they don't want to exist in their wonderful vision of the future. They want less work, a less messy office, fewer hostile customers and so on. As a result, vision can often be littered with negative expressions of what we don't want rather than what we do want. In motivational terms this is the difference between 'towards' and 'away from' motivation. The human brain struggles to think in negative terms because in order to 'not think' about something we first have to think about it. This phenomenon was popularised in the field of psychology as the 'Ironic Process' or 'White Bear Effect'[46]. Researchers found that the harder you try not to think about something the more it intrudes on your thoughts!

This issue is well known in psychology and has been studied extensively. Even as far back as the 1800's author and philosopher Dostoevsky observed:

"Try to pose for yourself this task: not to think of a polar bear, and you will see that the cursed thing will come to mind every minute." **Fyodor Dostoevsky, Winter Notes on Summer Impressions, 1863**[47]

In psychology this is known as the 'rebound effect'. In addition, many people find it harder to actively pursue the direction of a vision when it contains negative descriptions. It is far more helpful and effective to express what you want to see or what will exist. This enables people to actively work towards the goal and take positive steps.

Present Tense

This approach sometimes confuses people, but this is actually the most powerful technique and is almost unheard of in the companies I work with. You should create, and speak, your vision in the present tense, not in the future tense. By that I mean you must imagine yourself already in the future and describe what is happening around you, what you see, feel, hear etc. The use of present tense draws in the audience and brings a sense of immediacy to the vision.

Notice the difference between these two vision statements:

Statement 1: *In two years we will be in beautiful new offices with modern décor and the latest technology. We will be talking and listening to our customers about what they want us to be doing in the future. We will be spoken about in the media and people will be complimenting the flexible service we offer.*

Statement 2: *It is two years from today. We are in beautiful new offices with modern décor and all around us is the latest technology. We are talking and listening to our customers about what they want us to be doing in the future. People are speaking about us in the media and they are complimenting the flexible service we offer.*

You should be able to feel the difference between the first statement written in the future tense (we will be), and the second written in the present tense (we are). The second statement should feel more real and more tangible.

This technique might seem a little unusual, but once you become familiar with it your words and visions will stand out from the crowd!

Powerful Language

Much like storytelling, this is no place for tame language. If you want to tap into desire and really inspire people you must use language that has electricity or energy. Boring corporate language and tired clichés must be banished. The vision needs to be a treat for the senses, filled with sumptuous language and descriptions.

Don't say something has 'improved', instead say it's 'unrecognisable!'

Swap words like 'changed' or 'reorganised' for words like 'transformed'

By using unusual words and vivid language your vision statement will stand out from normal corporate communications. In addition, when you come to speak your vision it is easier to become passionate when the words are bigger and more descriptive.

Before writing this book I read and researched a number of organisational vision statements, and none reached the standard I believe is required to inspire people. This is unsurprising since an organisational vision must be relevant to a diverse population and also acceptable to the wider stakeholders, meaning any statement is likely to be heavily sanitised. The most powerful and compelling visions exist in teams and departments and this is where you should focus your efforts rather than challenging upwards.

Try to see vision as just another form of storytelling. You are telling a story about the future. The vision is painting a vibrant, engaging picture with words that bring your goals to life. Use all of the storytelling skills discussed in the previous section, including speaking with clear emotion. As previously mentioned, it can be uncomfortable to express emotions in an organisational context, and Collins and Porras readily acknowledge that some managers find this difficult, but they also believe that *"passion, emotion and conviction are essential parts of [a] vivid description."* It is precisely these ingredients that motivate others.

Although not strongly visual, these words by Apple's Tim Cook express a clear and emotional picture about the values, guiding philosophy and direction of the organisation:

> *We believe that we are on the face of the earth to make great products and that's not changing. We are constantly focusing on innovating. We believe in the simple not the complex. We believe that we need to own and control the primary technologies behind the products that we make, and participate only in markets where we can make a significant contribution. We believe in saying no to thousands of projects, so that we can really focus on the few that are truly important and meaningful to us. We believe in deep collaboration and cross-pollination of our groups, which allow us to innovate in a way that others cannot. And frankly, we don't settle for anything less than excellence in every group in the company, and we have the self-honesty to admit when we're wrong and the courage to change. And I think regardless of who is in what job those values are so embedded in this company that Apple will do extremely well.* **Tim Cook**[48]

Using word pictures to motivate beyond problems

As we have discussed, a well told story can fire our imagination and transport us into the world of the story. It allows us to leave our reality and imagine a new and different one. This can be especially useful when dealing with a frustrated or 'stuck' audience. When people face long-standing problems they often start to lose hope; they believe that nothing can be done and their motivation quickly dwindles. Creating word pictures using the vision techniques enables you to move people past the blockages into a different reality. It is a beautifully simple technique: firstly, identify the problem or source of frustration and then paint a picture of how the world might look if that problem was solved or removed.

For example, imagine I manage a team who consistently receive incomplete or inaccurate data from other departments. This has been happening for some time and team members have become cynical and they act negatively towards the departments involved. I've tried to address these issues using all the normal avenues but it has not had any significant impact on the situation.

I now want to re-energise the team to inspire them to look past these persistent problems. I might say:

> *"Imagine sitting at your desk on a Monday. You open up a programme that instantly displays all the data from the other departments. As you scan through the information you can see it changing because it is being updated live and automatically, so our departments are sharing the same information and no one has to lift a finger to get this information to us. You glance up at our team whiteboard to see the agenda for the week. On the schedule you see that there are three strategic review meetings with three different departments. These are new meetings we organise regularly so that we can listen to the needs of the other departments, raise questions and clarify information. We arrive at the Friday at the end of the month. Rather than being the last team to leave the office, we're finishing early at 4pm because our new team tradition is to spend an hour together socially at the end of every month to celebrate how hard we have all worked."*

This word picture uses all of the vision techniques: positive imagery, powerful language and present tense. It aims to inspire and energise the team using the power of desire. If they start to imagine life in the world I've described they will feel a sense of desire - 'I want that!'. With their emotions engaged in this way they will be willing, or even eager, to discuss the subject.

With an open-minded group you can work with them to create the picture themselves:

"What would it be like if this problem didn't exist or was solved? Describe what you would see/hear/feel?"

The technique is hugely effective.

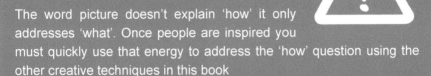

You must keep in mind the following limitations:

Whilst the word picture can be ambitious, it must feel possible within the audience's reality

The word picture doesn't explain 'how' it only addresses 'what'. Once people are inspired you must quickly use that energy to address the 'how' question using the other creative techniques in this book

The technique may not work if an audience feels powerless or does not trust you

I've drawn much from the work of Collins and Porras in this section so I will allow them the final words:

> *"The function of a leader - the one universal requirement of effective leadership - is to catalyse a clear and shared vision of the organization and to secure commitment to and vigorous pursuit of that vision"*[49]

5.6 The misunderstood role of fear in inspiration

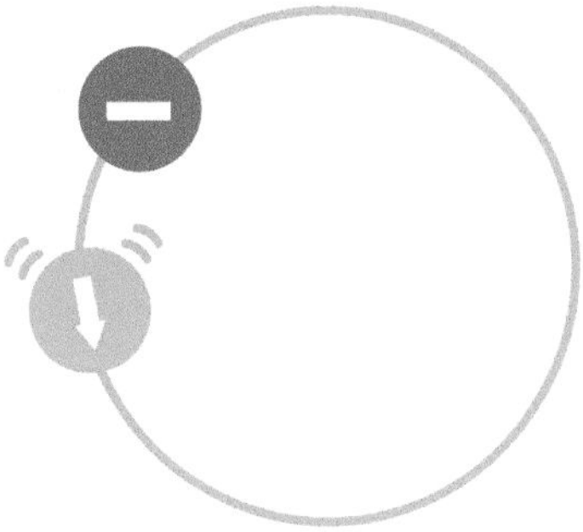

As mentioned in the introduction to this chapter, the role fear can play in inspiration is controversial. If you are uncomfortable with the following arguments, I encourage you to focus on the other techniques in this chapter instead.

In the previous section we discussed 'towards' and 'away from' motivations. Unsurprisingly, 'away from' motivation relates closely to the fear motivation. To explore the role of fear in inspiration we will take an unexpected turn and consider the second law of thermodynamics (bear with me on this one!). The second law essentially states that if you have an isolated system, any natural process in that system will increasingly cause disorder. This is known as *entropy.* Entropy can only be counteracted by the application of 'energy'. For example, a building would eventually collapse if it wasn't maintained by the input of energy via cleaning, painting, repairing and so on.

The concept of entropy also means that every natural process will follow the easiest path possible. In humans this manifests itself as laziness. Evolution tells us to rest as much as possible (i.e. take the easiest path) so that we're saving up as much energy as possible. In this way, entropy is the force that traps us in habits, routines, assumptions and reactions. In his book ***The Road Less Travelled,*** author M. Scott Peck[50] famously referred to all growth as effortful because it requires us to pit ourselves against the drag of entropy.

So what has this got to do with fear? Well, we all find ourselves falling into patterns of laziness. Most frequently these are habits and routines, things that we do almost without thought. It is far easier to maintain these patterns than to challenge and change them, unless we are motivated to do so. Fear is a hugely powerful emotion and in many ways provides greater urgency than desire, and in this way can be the motivational force to trigger a directional change or a shift in habitual behaviour. Think about people you know who have made profound changes to their life. My guess is that many of these changes started with a fearful shock of some description.

Fear can be useful to 'wake people' from sleepwalking through life, and it can be especially powerful when your audience has become complacent or stuck in some way. Some years ago I read a book called ***Business Beyond the Box*** by John O'Keeffe[51]. As I read the chapter called "Getting Demoralized by Incrementalism" I started to feel fearful, I even got angry. I wanted to argue with the author about the unfairness of those words he had written. The fear that it might be true really did inspire me to change my approach to business and as a result I become far more radical. Clearly it resonated with me, but this is a very personal matter and it may not resonate with you.

The chapter simply asked the following series of questions:

Next month . . . starts a new year . . . Is there any real point in us living that year or might we just as well go into a coma? . . . Will the world be any different for us having lived this year? Will we ourselves be any different, for the better, after the year is over?

You live in a box called a house - is it really so different from all the other boxes?

You travel in a box on wheels - is it really so different from all the other boxes?

You go to an office box - is it really so different from all the other office boxes?

At work, are we simply to live out a commonplace existence... just like millions of others in hundreds of other corporations, all in their own little boxes just like us, earning a wage to keep us alive until we're dead?

Are you dressed in a box called a suit, perhaps the same colour as all the other boxes, with perhaps an incremental difference of a wider stripe, or perhaps choosing a slightly different tie or a brightly coloured blouse - an incremental difference that you celebrate as a major distinctiveness?

Is what you do during a work day really just existing in a box of routines and habits established by others before you or around you ...?

Are things really, in the big scheme of things, going to be that much better for you acting out your life this day, this week, this month, this year?

Do you want to stay stuck in a rut? Accepting your state in life? Accepting where you are, what you have, what you do... ?

Business Beyond the Box: Applying Your Mind for Breakthrough Results

By John O'Keeffe

Did it make you feel uncomfortable? Did it upset you, or frustrate? If so, great, because it has generated emotions, and emotions are the starting point for inspiration. If it didn't have an effect on you try reading it again, slowly reflecting on your situation. This passage had a real emotional effect on me and I believe it is an example of appropriate use of fear. The author doesn't manipulate my emotions or do anything unethical. He simply asks some questions and my mind is forced to confront an uncomfortable reality, a reality that would be easier to avoid. The answers, and the fear, were entirely my own and as someone who felt a bit quirky because I wore brightly coloured ties the message really hit home! O'Keeffe concludes: *"Whatever job you do, whatever role you play, whatever life you lead, you can aim for step-change results within that job, that role, that life, rather than being content with just making it marginally better."* In many ways that is what sowed the seed that eventually brought me to writing this book. I wanted to tell you: be inspirational, do something different, be a leader!

How to work ethically with fear!

If you feel uncomfortable using fear to inspire, it might help you to see the present as the beginning of a fork in the road. When an audience leaves the room after you have finished speaking, they can move forward in one of two ways. They could go back to working the way they did before, integrating small elements of your guidance perhaps, but essentially making little meaningful change. Alternatively, they could take your words on board and make profound and meaningful changes to their working practice, resulting in a different direction or future.

Your role is to help your audience understand more clearly the implications of their decisions. Most audiences think in the here and now; they think of the future in terms of the next few weeks or months rather than years. If you can help them to see how the longer term future might look if nothing is to change, they may be inspired to change.

The process works through a problem or a concerning situation using questions built around ***IMPACT*** and ***EFFECT***. You will see how dramatic the answers become. When handled well, that drama can generate a sense of fear, motivating people to choose the desired path rather than risk the alternative.

In chapter 5.5 we imagined a team struggling with other departments consistently giving them incomplete or inaccurate data. Using this fork in the road technique, the conversation might go like this:

Speaker: *What is the impact of the poor data we are getting?*

Group: Tasks take more time than they should and we end up reporting inaccurate results to senior management

Speaker: *What effect is that having on our department?*

Group: It is making us look bad to senior management, and we are inconveniencing the other departments that we are constantly chasing

Speaker: *And what is the impact of that?*

Group: Well, some people say we are developing a reputation for causing problems and delays

Speaker: *If we, as a department, are unable to change the situation over the next few months, what do you think is the longer term impact?*

Group: People will lose trust in us, our stress levels will increase, and we'll keep missing key targets!

Speaker: *And so what effect would that have on you by this time next year?*

Group: I'd probably hate my job! We might be restructured, some of us could lose our jobs.

Speaker: *Thank you for your honesty. It sounds like we can't afford to be complacent about this issue. Clearly we need to take significant action right now to avoid those outcomes (Our fork in the road).*

This demonstration is a best case scenario for the conversation and, to be done effectively, the outcome in the real world would rely heavily on the facilitation skills of the leader (as we discussed in chapter 4). Alternatively, the subject could be approached in small discussion groups of 3-5 people, or it could be delivered as a formal presentation by the leader who would work through the argument themselves. This is high risk however, because you are assuming that the audience will agree with each impact and effect step. Regardless of how you navigate this area of inspiration it is critical that you always remain non-manipulative in your approach. You must focus your intentions on the needs of your audience and the best long term outcome.

CHAPTER SUMMARY

INSPIRATION

Inspiration is an emotion, therefore if you want to inspire people you must have a positive emotional impact on them. You must make them *feel* something. This isn't possible unless you visibly show emotions yourself.

AUTHENTICITY

Authenticity is at the heart of being inspirational and that is great news. The best way to inspire is to be yourself! That is easier said than done because the challenge is to drop all the masks and defences we normally wear and risk being vulnerable in front of our audience.

STORYTELLING

The quickest and most important route to empathy is through effective storytelling. When a story is well told the audience will put themselves in your position and feel what you felt. When telling a story remember to maintain authenticity and risk showing the real emotions, re-live the story don't re-tell it!

For references and links from this chapter visit chris-atkinson.co.uk/books

VISION:

Vision is our route to tapping into desire. The key to using this process is to be as vivid and as visual as possible. Describe the outcomes of whatever you are talking about in storytelling terms. Try starting with the word "imagine..."

FEAR

Fear can inspire people to change fast but we must be careful about how we use this knowledge. It is important not to manipulate either directly or accidentally. Help people see this moment as a crossroads and then through your presentation make real the possibilities if they were to take the 'wrong' path.

5

CHAPTER 6

HANDLING QUESTIONS & DISRUPTIONS

6.1 Why take the risk of Q&A?

Presenters can get extremely anxious about the question and answer period of a presentation. Not only should you welcome an opportunity for questions but you should actively encourage questions and discussion with the audience. Q&A is the ultimate in audience engagement; the audience is in control and *they* decide what they are interested in rather than the speaker.

There are risks involved, certainly. There is the chance that some people will use this opportunity to attack or challenge you. It is also possible that you could lose control of the group if the discussion is hijacked by a contentious issue. But your audience's concerns will not magically disappear once they leave the room. If they are not able to address them with you directly, they will discuss their concerns between themselves once they have left, by which point you have no control or influence. One way or another, those thoughts, worries or complaints will come out! You have two choices: either allow the concerns to be raised and discussed during a Q&A session which you are involved in and have influence over, or allow the discussion to happen after your session and blindly hope that the outcome is favourable.

Some years ago I was working on a leadership project with the UK production site of a multinational chemical company. During that time it was announced that the site would be significantly reduced in size and the workforce was likely to be cut by around 50%. As you can imagine, rumours rapidly spread around the site, morale suffered hugely and the situation quickly descended into chaos. It was arranged for a board member from the head office in the USA to visit the site to give a presentation to the workforce. I left the site the day before his presentation feeling very glad not to be in his shoes. There were a lot of angry people waiting to hear him speak, and he must have been expecting a hostile audience.

The only space large enough to hold this town hall style presentation was the canteen so, on the day of the presentation, they cleared all the tables from the canteen and set out about 300 chairs theatre style. They created a small raised stage at the front for the board member's presentation, with a projector and a screen. Unfortunately I wasn't able to see his presentation, but I was onsite the next day and I heard some quite incredible comments. People were commending him and his approach, saying "he seemed like a very genuine guy", "at least he was honest with us", "it's good to know where we stand". I was confused and speechless. I would never have imagined such a turnaround would be possible. It was as if this man had pulled off an incredible magic trick.

So how did he do it? Well, when he saw the stage and the PowerPoint set up, he immediately asked to remove the screen and projector because he didn't have a presentation. All he wanted was a flipchart and someone to write on it for him. The local leadership team were rather perplexed by this and wondered what on earth he had in mind. At the allotted hour all production on the site stopped and the workforce filed in. They sat waiting for the 'big boss from head office' to speak, many of whom intended to give him a piece of their mind. The director stood in front of them and said something like this: "I'm only here for a relatively short time, so I imagine that the best thing I can do to support you during this difficult process is to answer your questions as truthfully and as openly as I possibly can. Before we go any further, can you tell me what questions you need me to answer?" The audience shouted out their questions and a management team member wrote them on the flipchart. Some were practical questions and some were naturally very emotional, but all were written up. He then spent the next two hours answering the questions, creating a dialogue and demonstrating a clear empathic response to their situation.

Over the years I've witnessed a number of senior management presentations about restructures, plant closures or acquisitions. Usually they are bland, predictable communications, relying heavily on PowerPoint and commercial justifications which can mean little to front line teams. I've never seen anyone else do what this man did. He stood before his audience without a plan or an agenda and simply talked about all their interests and concerns. Whilst I'm not suggesting that everyone left enthused - the situation was still fairly grim after all - they did leave with a greater understanding and, more importantly, a greater respect for the man who had flown all the way from the head office to listen and talk honestly to them.

Do not underestimate the power or potential of a strong question and answer period. Here are my top 5 reasons to prioritise this time in your sessions:

Clarifies the message – The questions that are asked will tell you what parts of your message are unclear or confusing to the audience. The questions give you a valuable opportunity to clarify those points.

Reinforces key points – You may have seen politicians using this technique. Your presentation should include a few key points. After answering every question, you should link the answer to one of your key points to reiterate the fundamental messages.

Exposes resistance – If concerns or disagreements are expressed, this is the only chance you have to address them whilst you are in control.

Encourages audience interaction – Whenever you are leading the discussion you are either assuming you understand the interests of the audience or telling the audience what they should be interested in. Q&A puts the audience in control and you will quickly learn where their interests lie!

Provides opportunity to add evidence – This Q&A session gives you additional time and a further opportunity to influence your audience by bringing in extra evidence to add weight to your presentation. It is important to prepare more evidence than you plan to use so that it can be held in reserve for the Q&A section.

Questions and answers have the potential to sustain an audience's interest far more than your presentation because of the promise of participation and interaction. A wise person once told me:

Q&A is not something to get through, it is the thing to get *to*

6.2 Facilitating a powerful Q&A session

The skills we discussed in chapter 4 are essential to the good facilitation of a question and answer period. In addition, there are a few simple techniques you can use to make the session more effective and make you look more professional. The tips loosely follow the sequence from opening the session to receiving the questions:

1. **Do set a specific time limit** – This is particularly important if the questions become hostile or challenging. It allows you to refer back to the time allocated rather than digress further and further from the topic. Say something like "we have 'x' minutes for questions."

2. **Don't ask a closed question such as "does anyone have any questions?"**- Human beings are lazy (as we found in chapter 5.6) and the easiest answer to that question is "no". A closed question such as this will often be met with silence.

3. **Do ask an open question such as "who has the first question**?" - By assuming that there are questions someone should eventually speak up, even if you have to sit through an uncomfortable silence first. An expectant expression and raising your hand while asking the question shows the audience what to do next.

4. **Don't jump in with an answer immediately** – This is one of the most common mistakes I see. A presenter answers the question almost before the audience member has finished speaking, sometimes even interrupting the question to give the answer! Answering too quickly will annoy the questioner and nobody likes to be interrupted. Wait calmly until you are sure the person has finished, then pause before you start talking. Be aware of your body language while you listen to the question and ensure you maintain the parking position (see body language, chapter 2.3).

5. **Do repeat the question to the rest of the audience** – With larger group sizes in particular it is possible that not everyone will have heard the question. By repeating the question it will also help you with the next point...

6. **Do answer to everyone!** Another very common mistake. When answering a question, direct your answer to the whole audience, not just the person who asked the question. It is quite likely that other people in the group had the same or a similar question, and you want to engage the whole group in the answer and discussion. It is a good idea to check back with the original questioner at the end of your answer.

NB. *An exception to rule 6: If the question asked is particularly hostile, aggressive or concerning an issue you would prefer not to get into, you may choose to answer the questioner directly, maintaining eye contact predominantly with that person. This can help contain the issue and prevent it from 'spreading' around the room to the rest of the group.*

7. **After you answer a question, ask another open question** – such as "who has the next question?"
8. **As time starts to run out take control of the audience** - Say "who has the final question?" This manages audience expectation and allows you to draw a close to the conversation when the audience wants to keep questioning. You should, of course, offer to answer any additional questions offline once you have finished your presentation.
9. **Always close the question and answer by restating your close or conclusion** – as we discussed in chapter 1.6 about closing, your audience will remember the last things said in your presentation. If you reiterate your closing message at the end of the Q&A, this will be freshest in their minds, not the last question you were asked.

By encouraging questions you keep the audience engaged and offer them an active role. This makes the audience more involved, not only in your presentation, but in the ideas you are trying to 'sell' to them.

6.3 Techniques to handle tough questions

Although the following techniques will help you to facilitate a Q&A session, they are equally useful whenever an audience member interrupts you or throws in a question. I've been collecting and refining the techniques in this chapter over many years of struggles and challenges with hostile audiences. I've tested various different methods and slowly refined them to bring you this list. I've experienced huge discomfort and failures in the process so that (hopefully) you don't have to!

When it comes to answering questions, you may be preoccupied by your knowledge. You are in front of the audience because of your knowledge or expertise, so this is only natural. If you don't know an answer it is best to say so and, where possible, facilitate connecting that question with someone who is in a position to answer it. You must trust yourself and your experience here. The following techniques quite deliberately don't tell you *what* to say, only *how* to say it. They provide a structure for you to 'hang' your knowledge on so that you can answer clearly, succinctly and professionally. When you drift from these structures you will most likely lose clarity and start to ramble, so practise being disciplined!

The following techniques are listed broadly in order of effectiveness, with the first technique being the most effective:

Start with an example

"Let me give you an example..."

Does your mind ever go blank when you are asked a question? This technique has magical properties because the moment you finish saying these words an example will miraculously pop into your head! I can't explain how or why but it really is rather amazing.

Starting with a story or example adds weight and credibility to your answer because stories in this context are factual rather than subjective. It is essential that you do not give away your answer or personal opinion until you have completed the story. This forces the audience to delay their reaction until they have considered your case. Using stories encourages the questioner(s) to discuss facts and concrete experiences rather than opinions and speculation. In addition, as we discussed in chapter 5.4 on storytelling, if we tell the story effectively there is a strong chance of empathy. The audience should, regardless of their own views, have a greater appreciation for the reasoning behind your opinions.

Making it work effectively: Always locate your story in a **single, specific time and place.** In other words, 'when and where', don't generalise. As always, never ever make up a story and pretend it's real.

Past – Present – Future

"In the past_______ this was because______ but now_______ so in the future_______"

This technique is especially useful when you need to own up to something or admit that something has gone wrong. Firstly, you must explain the issues in the context of the time they occurred:

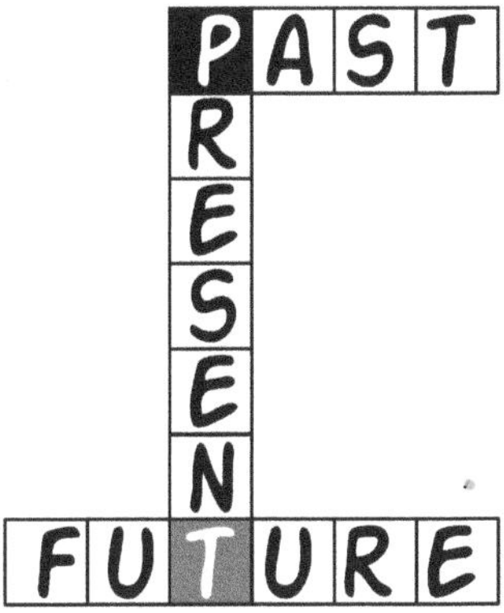

"In the past *admit issue(s),* this was because *specific things that created the situation*"

Then you need to discuss what changes have happened or are happening in order to correct the mistakes. These cannot be generic such as "now we're working harder", they must be concrete, tangible changes that have taken place since the initial problem:

"But now *specific changes that have happened*"

Finally, you must discuss the future in terms of how these changes will benefit the questioner (think - what's in it for me?). Essentially this section should be motivational for the questioner:

"So in the future *motivate/link to the benefits to the questioner*"

Making it work effectively: Surprisingly the 'past' referenced in the structure doesn't have to be a long time ago. Imagine I made a mistake yesterday, I might say: "yesterday I wasn't sufficiently focused on the project. This was because I put myself under pressure trying to do too many things for other people. This morning I spoke to those people and have told them I won't be able to help them until next week. So, for the rest of this week the project will have my full attention and I won't be making that mistake again."

Emphasise the positive

Often questions are challenging because they are considered from only one perspective. If you consider that many things in life follow Pareto's principle of 80/20[52], it is possible that the questioner is considering only the negative consequences (the 20%) of whatever you are suggesting, and ignoring the larger gains (the 80%). If you can help the audience see the positive outcomes rather than focusing on the negative you may be able to win them over. You need to remind them of the advantages and benefits that they may be overlooking.

Making it work effectively: A note of caution to ensure you use this in the appropriate situation. For some people the smaller negative 20% they are asking about is the single most important issue to that person. No matter how large or positive the other 80% of the consequences are, your answer will have little impact. For example, imagine my team face budgetary cuts and I end up losing my job to save costs. It is unlikely that I will be able to focus on the ways in which my redundancy will benefit the remaining team, no matter how numerous those benefits are. In this scenario, the only possible (and high risk) approach would be to emphasise the possible future options that are now open for me in my life!

Reverse it

"That's the very reason..."

I mentioned that this list was in order of effectiveness; this technique will only be effective in very specific circumstances. It works well when you want to show confidence, when the audience may have misunderstood the key point or when you want to shock your audience, but be warned, it is high risk! The technique is to essentially reverse the question to make a positive out of their implied negative.

Imagine I want to schedule a regular team meeting and someone complains that we don't have time. I might answer "that's exactly the reason why we need more meetings! We are not communicating with each other and we're working in silos. Consequently work is duplicated, which is wasteful and inefficient. By committing to an additional meeting we will save ourselves more time than we will lose."

A final technique:

Rephrase the question

"the question has to do with..." or "you're asking about..."

I would place this technique in the "in case of emergency" category. Use this technique if you find yourself having a strong emotional reaction to the question or questioner. The moment you feel your emotions kicking in you are compromised, no matter how hard you try to conceal it. Inevitably you will reveal your feelings through your body language, tone of voice or a cutting remark. Rephrasing the question gives you time to gather your thoughts, and enables you to take the 'sting' or 'barb' out of the question. By taking control of the question you can distance yourself from your emotional response and make it 'yours'.

It is critical that you don't change the meaning of the question. The technique works because it aims to depersonalise the emotional impact by identifying and answering the subject of the question. For example, imagine someone says "Senior management always lies to us and never tells the truth. Why should we listen this time?" Understandably this question may feel like an attack and may prompt an emotional response, but really the question is about trust, reliability or history and you should rephrase the question with these in mind. Say, for example: "Your question is about the level of trust with senior management", or "You're asking how this differs from previous occasions."

Health Warning: *As demonstrated by countless politicians, don't ever use this technique to dodge a question! After rephrasing a question you should always pause to allow the questioner to acknowledge they are happy you are answering their intended question. A simple nod is usually all I look for. Don't pause too long to wait for a response because they might interject with additional questions. There are links to some of these political moments in the chapter 6 resource section of the website.*

Tips for handling questions

- Predict objections to your case. Prepare likely questions and your answers, in advance
- Step forward with open gestures/a smile to welcome a question
- Maintain eye contact with the questioner until they finish. Pause before you answer
- Repeat or rephrase the question to show you've understood. This also buys you time to think
- When answering, look at the questioner 15% of the time and at others 85% of the time to involve the rest of the audience
- Keep answers short. Excessive justification reduces your credibility
- Guessing has the same effect. If you don't know the answer, say so – and offer to follow up later
- Don't waste the audience's time by answering irrelevant questions. But gain points by showing care – suggest where the questioner might find an answer

6.4 How to handle hostile people and digressions

Inevitably you will have the occasional challenging audience member set on disruption, and Q&A periods give them their opportunity to shine. They may try to score points or side-track your presentation for their own political or personal ends. Q&A sessions can be risky in this way but despite the risks, it is always worth encouraging questions because it demonstrates your open-mindedness and desire to build a dialogue.

Before we get further into this topic, let's establish three facts:

1. You **CANNOT** change or control people
2. You **DO NOT** want people to think like you
3. There will **ALWAYS** be some people who are unmanageable

It's not that people can't change, even if they seem stubborn and stuck in their behaviour, but there's a cardinal rule here that can't be ignored: no one changes unless they want to. Hostile, difficult people rarely want to. You might think that life could be so much more efficient and productive if we didn't have to deal with these kind of people, particularly now we are under so much pressure to strive and achieve. Imagine the time and emotional energy we'd save by not having all these frictions or pointless arguments. But this kind of thinking is fundamentally flawed and bad for our businesses. It is a seductive lie that promises the impossible - that life would be better and easier if others were more like us! Diversity of thought is essential for high performing teams and organisations, and there is a huge amount of research supporting that claim. Although there is no excuse for deliberatively disruptive or rude behaviour, you need this diversity of thought, no matter how uncomfortable it can feel.

The challenge for leaders and presenters is that no matter how hard we try to cover up our feelings, we are unable to fully conceal them. When we are affected by a challenging person, they and the entire audience will be able to see this. We are not as skilled as we think we are at hiding our frustrations. This can make us look unprofessional and in some scenarios encourage the audience to take sides. So it is important to first control and change our attitude to the person challenging us. This is easy to say, of course, but significantly harder to do!

Firstly, you must refocus your approach to people who are challenging. Instead of concentrating on what annoys you, try to direct your curiosity towards understanding their view of the world. This is another opportunity to use the questioning skills we discussed in chapter 5 about facilitation. Pose questions effectively to understand and expose what sits at the heart of the issue. If you take this questioning approach, you will appear interested rather than irritated.

The second step is a little harder. You must find a way to recognise and appreciate the talents and strengths the challenging person brings to the group. This is more of an internal recognition than anything stated verbally. You're probably thinking "but this person hasn't got any! They are a pain all the time!" This mindset perpetuates the problem, and since it is highly unlikely that that person will change to resolve the situation, you need to take command of your attitude. Maybe the thing that annoys you about that person would actually be considered a strength in a different situation. For example, that really negative person actually excels at technical problem solving because of their critical thinking. Or that aggressive person who always shouts is actually really passionate and always speaks their mind. You will be amazed what transformation can take place when you change your attitude and allow yourself to see the other person differently. This change is beneficial for both parties and encourages far more productive and positive communication.

When you are ready to respond to a challenging question, it is essential you acknowledge the practical and emotional needs of the other person. If you neglect one area you risk making the situation worse. Skilled facilitators recognise the part both head and heart play, and ensure their communication balances both. Once you have developed a curiosity about that person and have recognised the strengths they bring, you should be in a good position to answer their question in a collaborative and effective way.

You have the best chance of handling the situation if:

- You have a personal connection with the person
- You have earned their respect
- You aren't afraid or intimidated by the situation, and
- You are fairly equal in power (however you define it)

A final reminder: *Difficult people aren't going to change just to make you feel better. You are least likely to change someone's thinking if you're so angry, frustrated and fed up that you lose your composure and demand change.*

6.5 Moving beyond an apparent impasse

Occasionally you will encounter people who simply cannot be persuaded. They are inflexible and refuse to consider alternatives to their own viewpoint. You can lose a huge amount of time dealing with this kind of attitude and in doing so you risk losing the engagement of the rest of your audience. They need to be dealt with skilfully and tactfully to avoid weakening your position and to allow you to move forward with your agenda without causing offence.

The first technique to help you move beyond an impasse like this comes from the world of Neuro Linguistic Programming (NLP). This field of psychology considers how we can more effectively use our knowledge of the brain and of language to have greater impact and influence. NLP adopted the idea of 'chunking' from the world of computing; it simply means breaking things into appropriately sized bits. For a person to process information it needs to be in chunks of the right size – from the minute details right up to the bigger picture – whatever is appropriate for the person you are speaking to.

'Chunking' is a powerful concept and can move a conversation forward very effectively. When you reach an impasse or a disagreement in a conversation you can 'chunk upwards' until you find the point that you both agree on. Having reached an agreement on the topic, you can often move forward without needing to tackle the specific 'lower level' disagreement.

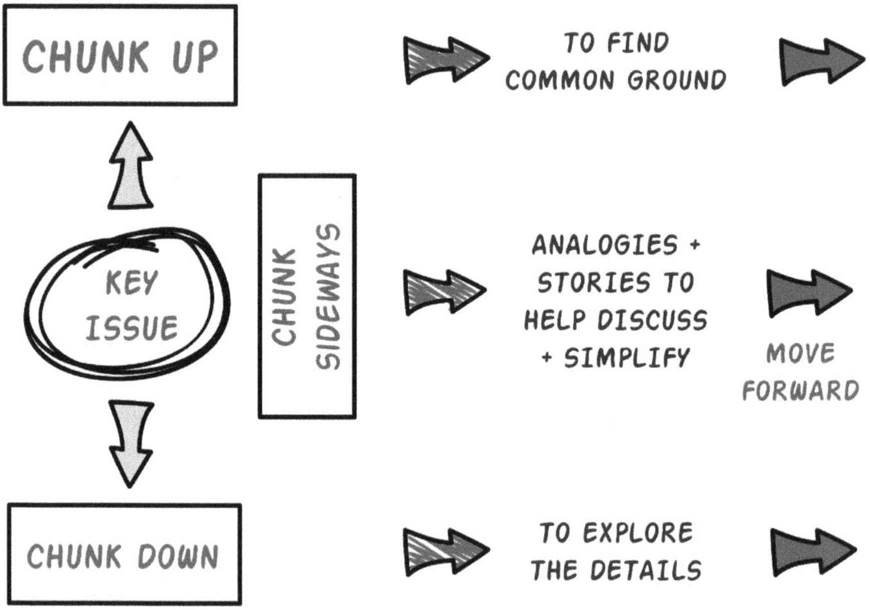

Let's revisit a conversation from chapter 5.6 as an example. The speaker will first try using the past-present-future technique before moving on to 'chunking':

***Speaker**: What is the impact of the poor data we are getting?*

Group: Tasks take more time than they should and we end up reporting inaccurate results to senior management.

***Speaker**: What effect is that having on our department?*

Challenging Individual: This isn't our problem. The poor data is coming from other departments.

***Speaker:** (using technique 'past-present-future') In the past that was the attitude that was often taken because we didn't have a strong sense of company culture. Now we are focused on operating as a single organisation and are working collaboratively on many projects. We don't want to let a silo mentality create barriers. This will mean that in the future other departments will be more considerate and supportive towards our needs as a department.*

Challenging Individual: Complete nonsense. They don't care about us and they never have. They give us poor data because they know we will deal with it. We need to give them a clear ultimatum.

***Speaker:** (recognising a possible impasse so chunking upwards) Regardless of where the responsibility or accountability lies, do we agree that our department is responsible for delivering the data to senior management?*

Challenging Individual: Yes, but we shouldn't be held responsible for other people's mistakes.

***Speaker:** (chunking upwards again) As the department responsible for data delivery, we must find the most efficient and effective way of accurately reporting that data.*

Challenging Individual: Yes of course, that is what I'm saying!

***Speaker:** (moving forward) That's good news. So let's focus on how we will report the data accurately. Your idea of challenging other departments is one option, but I also want to discuss other methods so that we can select the most efficient and effective method.*

Sensing an impasse in the conversation, the speaker chunks up to find the point of agreement. Once this agreement is found they are able to move forward. In this example, the impasse is the argument about who is responsible for the poor data. This could go round and round in circles, losing time and pulling more and more of the audience into the debate. By finding a point of agreement - *we must find the most efficient and effective way of getting that data accurately reported* - the speaker is able to move the conversation beyond this impasse.

In Neuro Linguistic Programming this chunking method is based on what is known as the 'The Milton Model'. It is a style of communication that moves upwards and focuses the ideas at a more generalised level. Conversely, there is a technique known as 'The Meta Model' which has a downward direction concentrating on very specific details. It is also possible to 'chunk laterally'. Stories or metaphors, for example, move sideways, maintaining the same level of detail but helping the audience to make new connections.

When a person is behaving stubbornly or creating an impasse, they may also try to steer the conversation off-topic or raise historical issues that are not directly relevant to the subject being discussed. In this situation you must maintain the focus of the conversation without appearing rude or dismissive. This involves significant facilitation and interpersonal relationship skills. From my many years as a speaker I have come to rely on a handful of lifesaving phrases. Here are some suggestions which you might adapt to use yourself:

That's an important question, and we shouldn't forget about it. Since it's not directly related to our desired outcomes for this discussion, could you make a note for it to be resolved later... (puts responsibility for further action back with the questioner)

Remember my role here is ... who else could you put that question to?

We don't have all the information to resolve that particular point here and now, how about we set some time aside to talk about that another day?

I can see you feel strongly about this but in the interests of time we need to stay focused on...

6.6 Overcoming silence

There may come a time when you open a Q&A session only to be met with total silence. So what do you do when there are (apparently) no questions? Let's be absolutely clear, silence does not mean there aren't questions in the audience's mind. Various social and environmental factors can cause silence. We have already discussed the value of a Q&A session and it is the presenter's responsibility to initiate it effectively by fully engaging the audience.

The most common error that results in silence is the way the speaker opens the Q&A period. In chapter 6.2 I introduced you to the main culprit: a closed question such as "does anyone have a question?" Invariably if you have a shy or quiet audience it is easiest and most comfortable for them to respond with silence or by actually answering 'no'. This closed question is often accompanied by two things:

- a tone of voice that suggests there *shouldn't* be any questions or that questions aren't expected

- a too short pause after asking the question, not allowing people to think and then ask a question

You must learn to use the phrase **"who has the first question?"** This is by far the best way to open and has an implication that questions are expected. Having asked this open question, the presenter must now muster all their confidence to withstand the silence that follows. Nine times out of ten, if you hold your nerve for long enough the audience will break the discomfort of the silence by asking a question. Sticking with this silence for long enough can be a real test of your self-confidence but it is worth it because once the first question has been asked you will often find the Q&A period will then flow naturally **("who has the next question?")**.

If you are working in an organisational culture where people feel less free to talk openly or might have concerns about saying what is on their mind, then you may find that even with the discomfort of the silence the audience still doesn't volunteer a question. As a presenter normally when I ask "who has my first question?" I wait until I feel uneasy with the silence, then count to five slowly. If at that point no one has said anything I can conclude one of two things i) there are no questions, or ii) the audience (for whatever reason) doesn't feel comfortable enough to ask a question. Once again I would emphasise that Q&A is too important to assume the reason is the first point, especially if there is some possibility of the second! We therefore may need to get the process 'jump started' and demonstrate to the audience that it is a safe and comfortable environment to ask questions. Start by saying **"one thing I'm often asked"** or **"a question I thought you'd ask"**. You then proceed to ask yourself a question. Make sure the question you ask yourself is something that is interesting, real and potentially challenging. This emphasises to the audience the level to which they can ask questions. If you ask yourself a tough question do make sure to prepare a strong answer!! You would look pretty foolish if you asked yourself a question you couldn't answer wonderfully.

After answering your own question you can then say **"who has my next question?"** and hopefully the process will then flow naturally. I wouldn't recommend asking yourself more than two questions.

Recently I was working in Japan for the first time with a multinational automotive company. Before I spoke, the President and CEO of the division was asked to deliver a brief introduction to the topic and answer any questions from the audience. He opened the Q&A session and was met by total silence. After what felt like an eternity he tried to engage the group, asking, "Who would like to be more involved in the creation of our strategy for the Japanese market?". Again, total silence.

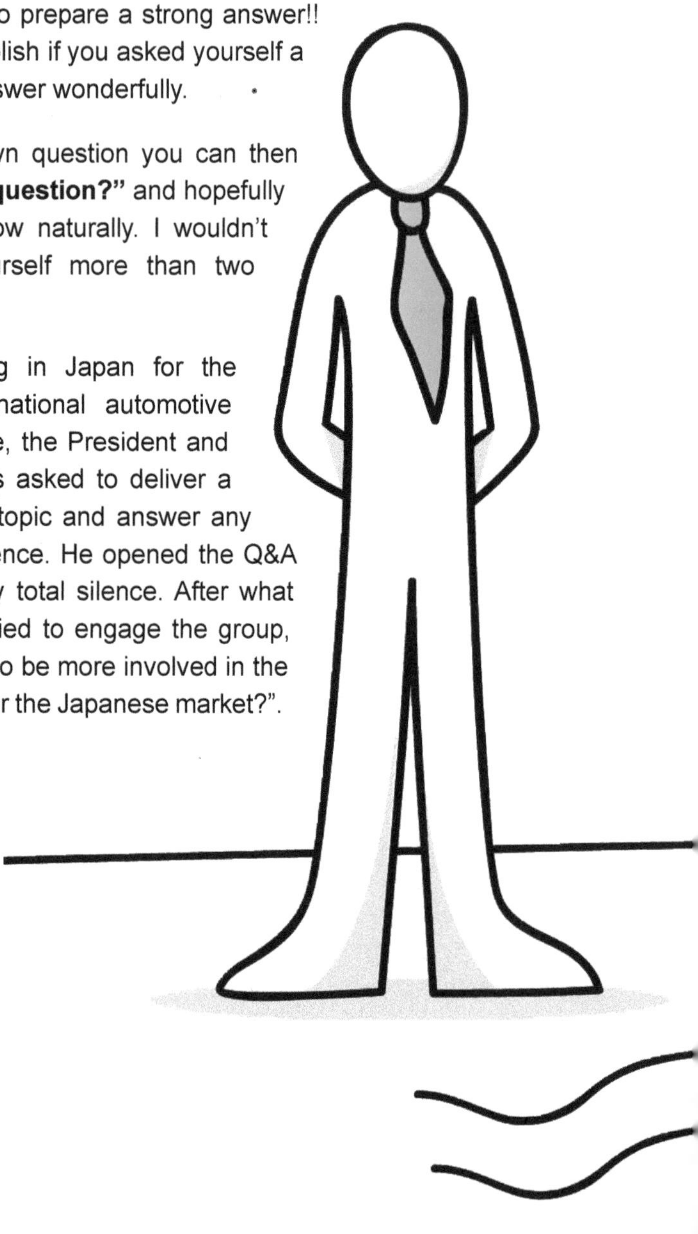

Eventually he gave up and sat down next to me. He leant over looking disheartened and quietly said, “So not one person in this group wants to support me or get involved? I thought It was such a great opportunity”. I worked with this same group over a number of days and the pattern of silence continued despite my best efforts. In time, as I came to better understand the culture, I realised that conversation flowed much more easily in smaller groups. I discovered that if I created small groups and gave each group a flipchart on which to write any questions, every single group would write **SOMETHING** down on the flipchart paper after some private discussion time! I could then stick their flipcharts on the wall and answer their questions.

By the end of the week we had created a process that really worked. I thought back to the CEO and his feeling that no one cared; this absolutely wasn’t true. There were opinions and questions in the group but, essentially, the facilitator had to find the right way to elicit them.

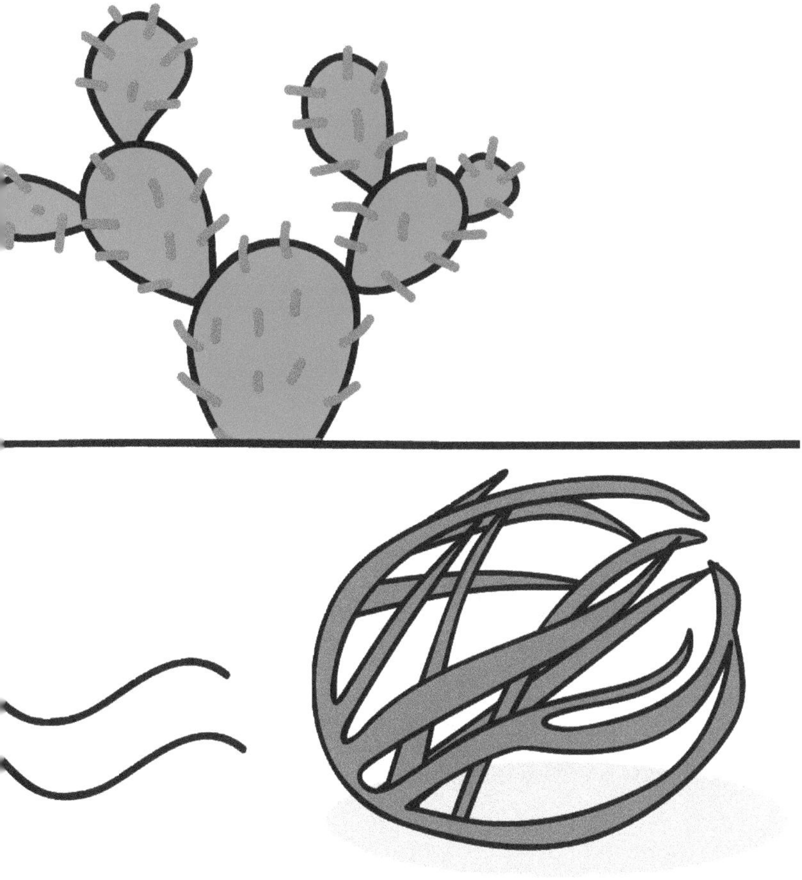

CHAPTER SUMMARY

TAKE THE RISK

Question and answer is not something to get through, it is the thing to *get to!* It is the point where the audience are able to truly focus on their needs and interests. It is a critical and valuable use of your time.

FACILITATION

Set a time limit and direct your answers to everyone not just the questioner. Remember to swap the phrase 'does anyone' with 'who' so that you ask "who has the first question?" and "who has the next/last question?" After that just wait patiently and be comfortable with the silence.

HOW TO ANSWER

The four techniques to answer are i) Example, use a story ii) Past present future, illustrate how the present differs from the past and the benefits in the future iii) Emphasise the positive, focus on the 80% of good rather than the 20% of problems iv) Reverse it, that is the very reason why we should. Additionally, when you have an emotional reaction you should rephrase the question first.

HOSTILE PEOPLE

Don't try and change the other person. The most effective technique to handling a hostile audience is to build a stronger relationship by working to understand their perspective (no matter how different from your own it might be!). Only by demonstrating that you understand their perspective do you have a chance of influencing them.

IMPASSES

When you reach a sticking point in the Q&A session, perhaps a point that the audience can't let go of or something that an individual will not shift their viewpoint on, you can use chunking. By chunking up (moving to a more general perspective) you can find where you and the other party agree.
From there it is easier to move forward.

For references and links from this chapter visit chris-atkinson.co.uk/books

SILENCE

The first challenge for the presenter is to become more comfortable with silence than the audience! The audience is equally as uncomfortable as you are, often this discomfort helps people break the silence and ask a question. If no questions are forthcoming ask yourself a question (and answer it).

6

CHAPTER

7

USING 'TECHNOLOGY'

My definition of technology in this chapter differs from the normal understanding of the word. Generally speaking, technology refers to electronic devices, but the 'technology' of an engaging and inspirational speaker is often much more low tech. I will use both definitions in this chapter.

Most people assume there is little to say about the correct usage of what is essentially office stationery and consequently the subject tends to be overlooked. This is a huge and costly mistake because effective use of all of the available technology (both digital and physical) can significantly increase your impact as a speaker.

7.1 Slides

If you have read the introduction to this book, you might be expecting me to dissuade you from using slides, but that is not necessarily the case. Chapter 1.7 details the legitimate reasons for using slides, so if you are creating a slide to satisfy one of these reasons, I believe their use is justified. Slideshows can be a fantastic addition to your presentation toolkit and can make your content more memorable, but you must resist certain temptations. As I said in the introduction: We can't expect software and slides to engage or inspire. If anything, technology is likely to hamper your efforts to engage. For many, less experienced presenters it is a *challenge to overcome,* rather than a tool to enhance. In the words of Edward Tufte.[53]

"Power Corrupts. PowerPoint corrupts absolutely."

During a leadership training programme for a well-known multinational company, we had scheduled a one-hour section for a senior manager to discuss organisational strategy with the participants on the programme. The group had little exposure to senior management so this was a hugely important communication. The senior manager arrived during the coffee break and immediately started preparing his laptop and making last minute alterations to his presentation. Instead of using this opportunity to connect with his audience, to chat and build rapport, to perhaps find out what they had been learning in the training programme, he appeared aloof and separate from the participants, fully engaged in his own task.

He began his presentation by handing out printed copies of his slides to the audience. I sat at the back, watching and at first thought little of it – if only I had taken a copy of that handout, I might have realised what was to come! By about 15 minutes into his presentation the audience was finding it hard to sustain interest. In that short period he had talked non-stop and covered 18 slides of dense, technical information. I assumed the audience must have seen these slides previously because they couldn't be expected to grasp all the complex details in less than 60 seconds per slide. I discretely took a copy of the printed presentation from a nearby table and to my horror I saw the full presentation consisted of 55 slides of technical data. Many audience members were reading ahead in the notes whilst he talked; the remainder had given up and resigned themselves to their fate. I later learned that the group had no previous knowledge of the majority of the information presented.

For the majority of the group that entire hour was a total waste of time, making it a very ineffective use of the senior manager's time.

The one-way delivery meant people were discouraged from asking questions and there was no audience interaction. This senior manager had a valuable hour with a key leadership level of his organisation, but instead of engaging with them and creating a dialogue, he lectured them. If fate had intervened and granted us a power-cut in the meeting room, I believe this same manager would have reverted to a much more genuine and approachable method of communication and talked to the group like a normal human being. Technology corrupts good people.

People process information in many different ways, as we explored in chapter 3.2, and the most engaging presentations are those that provide something for everyone. In particular slides appeal to visual-spatial intelligence. We know that people retain information better when they hear and see information at the same time but bullet points are not the most helpful visual material! Strong, clear pictures, graphs, and imagery work more effectively than bullet points in terms of visualisation.

Research by Richard Mayer at the University of California[54] provides evidence that might make you reconsider your approach to visual data. Mayer compared teaching material for various mechanical and scientific processes such as how a bicycle pump works and how lightning forms. He compared lessons that used only words with lessons that used words and pictures together. He found an average gain of 89% on knowledge transfer tests from learners who studied with text and graphics compared to learners who followed text-only lessons.

So far so good for our use of slides. Here is the problem; when additional, extraneous details were added to the visual material it was found to impair learning. Such additions were called "seductive details". Mayer found learners who studied the basic lessons learned more than those who studied from the enhanced versions which included these "seductive details". The average gain was 105%. He concluded that the more information you put on a visual slide, the more likely it is to *decrease* learning, understanding and recall.

This leads us to the first key message:

Self-explanatory slides

If you can email your slide deck to somebody so that they can read through them and see everything they missed, then your slides are self-explanatory. This is not a good thing. Many presenters assume a slide that can be understood in their absence is a good slide. If your slides are self-explanatory, the presenter isn't necessary. Moreover, if your slides are self-explanatory it is likely that a) they contain too much information and/or b) anyone not present to read them from the screen with the rest of the audience will feel disengaged.

Under these circumstances it is far better to send your slides in advance of your presentation along with a request for the audience to arrive prepared with questions. Your presentation now becomes a facilitation and Q&A session rather than a long lecture. In the academic world this is known as 'flipped classroom.'[55]

Designing great slides

Aim for 6x6

6 bullets per slide

6 words per bullet point

This is a **MAXIMUM** rule. Over the years, there have been many 'rules' for the best design of bullet points on a slide. All of these emphasise that less is more: the more you write the less the audience will take from your information. Keeping to 6x6 as a maximum rule will keep you in the safe zone, anything less is also good. For every additional word of bullet point you will be decreasing the effectiveness of your slide. If you believe the content of your slide is important, then it is important that people process and remember the information!

10 Seconds

A long established psychological principle tells us that it takes just 7 seconds to make a first impression. This is much quoted in the press in the context of job interviews and presentations. The same principle is broadly true for the 'first impression' of your slide. When they first see a slide, the audience quickly makes certain calculations. In line with the first impression principle, you have around 10 seconds before they make their vital decisions: Does this slide interest me? Is it complex or simple? Do I care?

Make sure the information on your slide can be rapidly processed. If a complex slide is absolutely necessary, consider building up the complexity using animations.

36 Point font size

The issue of font size generates a lot of discussion and debate. There are plenty of guidelines for minimum font size but most of the literature misses an absolutely critical point: presentations happen in a wide variety of meeting rooms using a wide variety of screen sizes. For that reason, it is impossible to give a single rule for all circumstances. My biggest concern is the growing use of wall mounted televisions as a replacement for projectors. Even the largest televisions are significantly smaller than the beam of an average projector. To stay consistent with the previous two points I recommend 36 point font size. This is the best size for a variety of room sizes and is still comfortable to read on an average sized television screen.

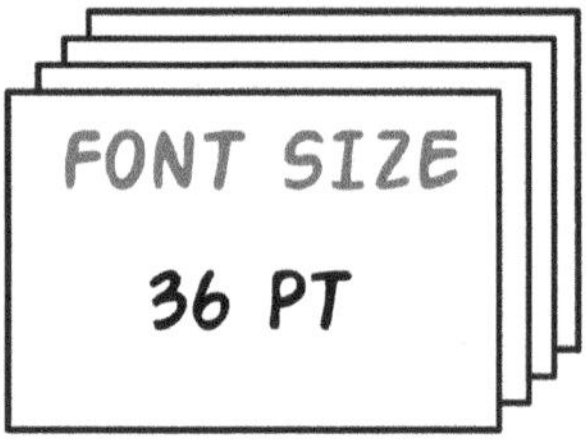

You can go smaller, but I encourage you to **NEVER USE** the shrink font button. If you find yourself hovering over that button, stop. Consider whether you can reduce the content or display the information differently. In other words, do anything rather than shrinking the font size!

Visualise text

If there is too much text or too many bullet points on your first slide, it will negatively impact your presentation. In the first 10 seconds your audience will already be tuning out, having deduced that it is going to be boring. Much of this argument has been covered in preceding sections, but essentially slides should add a visual aid to your speech - so make them visual! Very often, words can be replaced by imagery. Research shows that people remember images far more clearly than text. Avoid clipart images that have been around for years, these will only decrease your credibility and hinder memory retention. Photographs or bespoke graphics are much more professional and powerful.

Too many slides

MAXIMUM!
1 SLIDE EVERY
5 MINUTES

...but how many is too many? The oft quoted 'one slide per minute' is total madness. For most people working in organisations, following that rule would be professional suicide. The vast majority of professional slides are both content and data rich so it is unrealistic to expect an audience to process the information, engage with its meaning **AND** commit it to memory whilst listening to a presenter talk, all within 60 seconds. Furthermore, battering your audience with a slide every minute will kill audience engagement and attention levels.

Assuming your slides are 'normal' slides with bullet points, graphs, statistics and so on, you should aim for a maximum of **1 slide every 5 minutes**. If your presentation is longer than 60 minutes, I would encourage you to have 1 slide every 10 minutes.

The Exception: One slide per minute is conceivable if your slides are full screen pictures or huge single words. This concept has been popularised by the technique of PechaKucha[56]. Presenters create 20 large, bold slides which advance automatically every 20 seconds (20 slides x 20 seconds). This style of slide technique is attention grabbing, memorable and motivational, but sadly for many organisations it simply isn't practical for everyday presentations. It is great when it works, but it does require both careful preparation and creative thought.

7.2 Sticky notes

A whole section devoted to sticky notes? You're probably thinking one of two things: either that I'm a little crazy, or that you have already mastered the complexities of this particular piece of engagement technology. Whilst the first statement may well be true, I suspect the second is most likely false. Sticky notes are ubiquitous - they are in every meeting room and training room throughout the world and consequently I have seen a lot of people using them. I've concluded that most people simply haven't thought about their potential or the creative ways in which they can be employed.

Sticky notes are often referred to as Post-it® Notes, but in the interests of fairness, and sometimes cost savings, I must emphasise that many other brands are available. Sticky notes are wonderful things: they are simple to use, versatile, and can engage groups by encouraging interaction. They are quite possibly the easiest and cheapest item available to you in your engagement toolkit. This section will turn you from a basic level sticky note user into a professional!

Let's start with the basics...

Peeling

How do you peel off a sticky note once you have written on it? If you feel this is a silly question or is something you've never considered, it is possible you've been doing it incorrectly all your life. As an experiment, find a pad of sticky notes right now, write some notes on a few of them and peel them off. Stick those notes onto something near you so you can refer back to them in a minute. Do this now before you read on.

Give it a go before reading on!

The incorrect, but the most common, way to peel sticky notes is to pull from bottom to top. In other words, you peel the note upwards in a vertical motion. This results in the sticky part of the note curling. This curl has negative consequences for a facilitator. Firstly, less of the glue is in contact with the surface it is adhered to, meaning it is less able or likely to stick. Even if it initially sticks, it will fall off more quickly than a properly peeled note. Secondly, and more significantly, this curling effect makes the note point upwards, making it difficult to read and impossible to photograph. Since sticky notes are mostly used as visual references for groups to share their thoughts and ideas or information, it is imperative that they are clearly visible and legible.

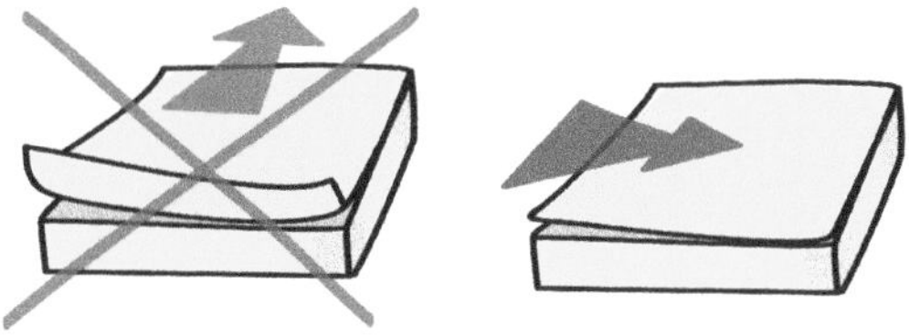

Sticky notes should be peeled horizontally from left to right or right to left. This prevents the curling and will allow the note to lie flat against any surface it is placed on. If you peeled some sticky notes earlier you can now check how you performed. Are they curling upwards? Try contrasting the two peeling techniques to underline the difference. You can now impress your colleagues with this unique knowledge.

Pens

The sticky note must always be paired with a marker pen. *Never* use sticky notes without also sourcing the appropriate number of marker pens. As we have discussed, sticky notes are primarily used to display information. If you don't provide marker pens (and often even if you do) audience members will start writing with a normal ballpoint pen. A normal pen simply won't be legible against the colour of the note because it is too thin and doesn't have the required contrast. Even when people appreciate the need for a marker pen they are likely to simply grab whatever is available in the meeting room, but in 99% of meeting rooms there is only one type of pen - the flipchart marker pen. More specifically, they are usually green or red flipchart marker pens! Red and green marker pens should be avoided whenever possible. The colours don't contrast enough on the sticky note and they cause issues for people with colour blindness. In addition, flipchart markers generally have very thick nibs so any writing on the traditional small sticky note is cramped and illegible.

The answer is quite straightforward - you need to use marker pens similar to the best known brand *Sharpies*. These pens have thinner, sharper nibs that allow you to write clearly and legibly onto a sticky note. Avoid the lighter colours and use strong, dark colours such as black, blue or purple.

Sizes

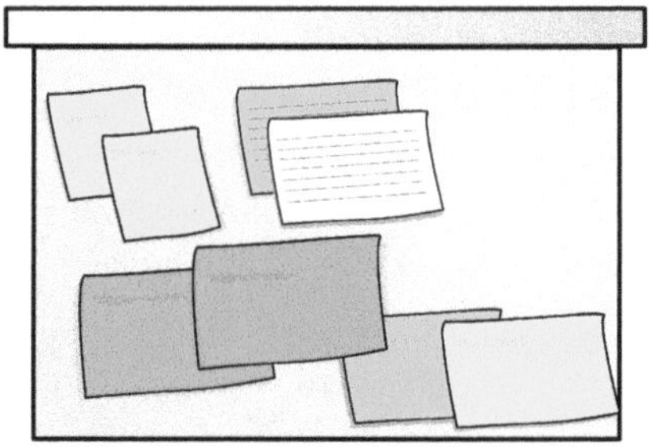

Have you ever considered the size of the sticky notes you use? The vast majority of notes in offices and meeting rooms are the standard square size 76mm x 76mm. Although you can purchase sticky notes in a variety of wonderful shapes, sizes and, as we will discuss later, colours. The task you assign your audience will dictate the size of sticky note required. You can't just throw any size sticky note pad to your audience - no no no! Sticky notes are most commonly used to visualise information from a group so that everyone can read it. If you use a standard sized square sticky note, how much information can be written on it and remain clear and legible to a group from a distance? The answer is approximately one word. If your task involves single word answers then the standard sticky notes will work perfectly. For example, if you ask your group to "*list the characteristics of a great leader*", most responses will be single word answers.

Now imagine you ask your group to "*describe the problems you face in dealing with customers.*" You are more likely to receive longer, more detailed responses and these will not work on a standard sticky note. Instead, you will need a much larger sticky note so that the group can write a few words or sentences. Sticky notes go all the way up to A5 in size. Using a note this big can bring a nice sense of drama and even allows you to use flipchart marker pens (but only with these super-sized sticky notes!).

Tip: Always ensure you give the following instruction before your task and before audience members start using the sticky notes:

"Using the marker pens provided, write one idea per sticky note..."

I promise you that if you omit this (and sometimes even if you don't), some people will use ballpoint pens and others will write a list of bullet point answers, all on one sticky note.

Colour

> **Caution:**
>
> Don't ever enthuse to your audience about how cool it is to have different colour sticky notes!
>
> Be cautious about colours that are too dark to write on clearly (e.g. red or purple)

One of the most boring, uninspiring and downright unimaginative things you can do as a facilitator is to provide only yellow sticky notes. Yes, they're functional and yes, it's still a lot better than delivering a slideshow of a hundred slides, but you can do SO much better. Sticky notes can tap into the creativity and energy of a group, but using a uniform industry-standard yellow sticky note stifles creative energy and makes the end result look uninspiring and pedestrian. Using a mixture of colours makes the end result far more vibrant and visually interesting. It's a small change but it can make a huge difference.

The different colours can play an important role in the design of your activities. For example, you can employ a traffic light coding system, such as:

"On the green sticky notes write down what helps you perform well in your role, on the yellow notes write things that concern or worry you, and on the pink notes write any problems you face that prevent you from working effectively."

(N.B. I avoid the use of red because it is too dark too write on).

Colours can be used to assign categories, or different groups can be given different coloured sticky notes so you are able to see which ideas came from which group. This is useful when debriefing and it also allows you to gauge the productivity and engagement levels of each group.

Creative use of sticky notes

We've explored the most obvious uses for sticky notes but with some creative thought there are an infinite number of ways to include them in your meeting, training session or workshop. For example, sticky notes can be used to:

- Vote on ideas by sticking them against the preferred idea
- Traffic light suggestions (green = good, amber = not sure, red = concerns)
- Create large patterns and shapes
- Stick on people for the purposes of a game or activity (extra sticky needed)

There are a variety of different shaped notes available. I recently bought a pack of 'first-aid' themed sticky notes that were shaped like plasters, bandages and antiseptic cream. I could perhaps use these in a health and safety workshop to stick against ideas generated by the group. I have also used sticky notes shaped as:

- Large hands
- Outline of a person
- 'Thumbs up' gesture
- Pre-printed arrows saying "great idea", "to do", "what if", "more of this"

7.3 Flipcharts

Unlike sticky notes, flipcharts have few hidden complexities and function as you would expect. The following guidelines will help you appear more professional, as well as making life easier for your audience:

Write big – There is little point writing something on a flipchart if no one can read it! Your text needs to be comfortably read from the back of the room; generally this means writing larger than you think is necessary.

Write in lower case and avoid joined-up writing – In some ways this is about channelling your inner 5-year-old. Research has demonstrated that lower case text is easier and quicker to read. Of course, this doesn't mean that your handwriting will be! So when you write, use capitals only for the start of sentences or proper nouns, avoid joined-up writing and keep the letters large and separate.

Use lined paper if possible – Lined flipchart paper can make a huge difference to the neatness of your finished flipchart. The lines are nearly invisible to your audience but your writing will be straighter and more consistently sized. A lined flipchart filled with text will look much more professional than an unlined one. If clear writing is important and you don't have lined paper you could also pre-line your own flipchart pages lightly with pencil in advance of the session or workshop.

Use green and red pens only as accent colours – I mentioned this in the previous section on sticky notes. Red and green do not contrast well on paper and are surprisingly hard to read from any distance. In addition, anyone with red/green colour blindness will struggle to read the text. Write with strong dark colours and only use red or green as an accent colour to underline or draw around your text.

Learn some simple drawings – Text only flipcharts are painfully dull. Drawings add visual interest and make your content more memorable. You're possibly thinking, "I can't draw!" Well no, neither can I. I looked to more artistic people for inspiration and practised a lot, and I now have a limited ability to draw people, boxes, houses, computers etc. This isn't about your artistic ability; it's about learning to make a few recognisable shapes to illustrate your words. The result is well worth the effort!

Question why you are writing on the flipchart – I was recently at a training event where we discussed business strategy. The facilitator asked questions such as: "what are the strengths of the organisation?", "what are the weaknesses?", "what changes do we anticipate in the industry?" and so on. The answers were meticulously written up on a number of flipcharts. After those questions the conversation moved on to other themes. The flipcharts were not referenced again, nor were they used for any other activities, and after the event they were thrown away. This struck me as a waste of time and a real missed opportunity.

At the very least, flipcharts and important work should be photographed and circulated to participants after the event.

Flipcharts can be used far more productively by:

- Referencing the content during the remaining presentation
- Dividing up the content between audience groups for further discussion
- Getting the audience to link together different pieces of flipchart content
- Returning to the flipchart for further activities and work, adding ideas etc.
- Summarising the session using the flipchart content

Often people habitually record everything on a flipchart without considering their reasoning or methodology. Save a lot of time and effort and only use a flipchart if you plan to refer back to it or to use it again.

Make the audience do the work

This is especially important if you are facilitating a group on your own.

To facilitate effectively your focus must be with your audience so that you can form the right questions, guide the conversation and, when necessary, challenge statements. If you are writing things on a flipchart your attention and your eye contact is taken away from the audience. This causes many facilitators to 'talk to the flipchart' and at the same time they write more quickly and less legibly. Frequently there are uncomfortable silences whilst the audience waits for them to finish writing. This interrupts the natural flow of conversation and is detrimental to the session.

Caution:

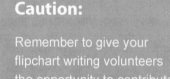

Remember to give your flipchart writing volunteers the opportunity to contribute their ideas. You may need to ask them directly (spotlight technique) to make sure they are included in the conversation.

When you are the sole facilitator it is far better to ask for an audience member (or two) to write up what is being said. If it is a quick-fire brainstorming session, having two writers can really help. You are then free to focus on your audience and the conversation can flow at a natural pace whilst someone else records everything.

7.4 Videos

At my secondary school there was a long standing joke that if a teacher didn't have a lesson plan they would simply put on a video, dim the lights and make us watch an 'educational' film - normally of dubious quality. We loved it because we could switch our brains off (we rarely learnt much from these videos, nor were they ever debriefed or discussed in depth). In the same vein I think people sometimes used videos and film clips as a substitute for the work they should have done themselves to engage the group. Times have changed significantly since my school days and the video content on sites such as YouTube is an everyday part of life for most people. Video production has also improved and there is a huge amount of outstanding information freely available online.

If you want to use a video in your workshop, meeting or training session there are a few things to keep in mind:

- **Keep it under 5 minutes** – if you use anything longer it is likely your audience will start to lose interest. The only exception to this is if the clip is educational, heavily informative or detailed in content e.g. a documentary. Under these circumstances it is possible to use clips of up to 15 minutes, but I would caution going any longer than this.
- **Have good speakers** – it looks very unprofessional if the audience cannot hear the sound or if you are using laptop speakers (which are rarely good enough quality). Invest in a good, portable speaker.
- **Download rather than stream, if legal to do so** – the last thing you want to have to worry about when you are leading a discussion is whether your internet connection is working. Assuming you are not in breach of any legal conditions associated with the clip, it is always better to download the video to your computer so it is guaranteed to play smoothly.
- **Be cautious around humour** – this has been mentioned throughout the book but it is worth repeating. Something you find funny may not appeal in the same way to your audience, or they may deem it 'inappropriate'. Please tread carefully when using 'funny' videos; check with trusted colleagues and use good judgement.

Powerful videos can make great openings for presentations. A video used in an opening should be especially short so that it grabs the audience's attention before you step in to deliver the remainder of the opening. Videos can also provide evidence in support of your message; look for something credible with a direct relevance to your message. Finally, videos can also be used to provide an inspirational, uplifting close. If you decide to use a video for your closing, remember you must also have the last word (as we mentioned in chapter 6.2). Once the video ends ensure you have a short, clear closing statement to end the session.

If you decide to use a video clip ensure that the moment the video finishes you are ready to bridge into a pre-prepared discussion/explanation with the audience about the meaning, relevance and implications of the video. This maintains the flow of your presentation and shows the audience that your choice of video was carefully chosen and considered.

7.5 Other interactive technologies

In addition to the obvious facilitation 'technology' regularly found in meeting rooms (projector, sticky notes and flipcharts), I've discovered a few others over the years that have helped me stand out as a presenter and facilitator. These items can increase your creativity and make you significantly more memorable for your audience.

Electronic voting

There are many variations of this idea using different technologies. Allowing an audience to participate by voting on various topics is a great way to get them involved and engaged in a session. It is most commonly used with survey-style questions. You can, for example, ask questions about staff morale levels (are they 'low, medium, high'), or ask the group to select work priorities. The anonymity of the voting allows more sensitive subjects to be investigated. Once everyone has voted the results are immediately displayed onscreen in whatever form you choose. This gives a skilled facilitator real data, context and evidence to work with. It can also be used to harvest simple data.

Creative facilitators can use this technology in different ways, such as competitive quizzes.

The technology for voting falls into two basic categories:

- Handheld voting devices (like a small remote control) with a few simple buttons
- App based voting using personal smartphones

The dedicated handheld voting devices are easy to use and reliable, but they are expensive. The app based solutions are cheaper but require all participants to have the app and to be online.

Table top flipcharts

Very often when groups are asked to work on a particular activity, the facilitator tears off a sheet of flipchart paper for each group to work on. Almost immediately there is chaos as tables are cleared or moved to create a space for the flipchart paper. It is actually quite hard to write on a piece of flipchart paper when it is lying flat. You sometimes see the designated writer on their hands and knees on the floor because that is the only place where they have the space to write comfortably on the paper.

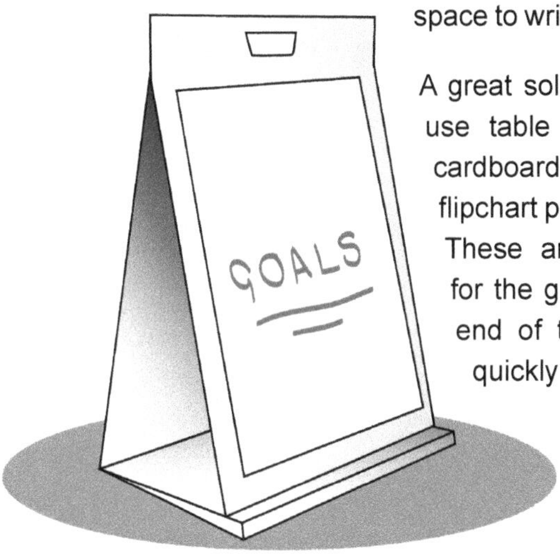

A great solution for these issues is to use table top flipcharts. These are cardboard stands with sticky-backed flipchart pages, like giant sticky notes. These are much more convenient for the group to work on and at the end of the activity the pages can quickly and easily be stuck up on the wall. They are lighter and cheaper than large flipchart stands and far more practical.

Links to many of the items in this section are available on the website in chapter 7 resources

Static paper

Magic whiteboard™ is the leading brand of this technology, but you can find similar products with different names. Essentially it is plastic whiteboard material which comes on a 'tear off' roll. The sheets have a static charge which enables them to stick to virtually any surface. This means they can be moved and repositioned around the room as if they were magnetic. Because of this flexibility, this technology is perfect for small meeting rooms or if you have to carry your own materials. You can find these in a variety of sizes from standard sticky note size up to flipchart-sized pages.

Additionally, unlike paper, there is no risk of the ink bleeding through to the surface beneath so you can write directly onto the sheet against a wall or window without the worry of leaving marks.

You can use these just as you would use a flipchart but creative people can find other uses which take advantage of the static nature of the material. For example, I have written various discussion points on a sheet, cut it into pieces to create a kind of jigsaw and tasked groups with putting the content in the correct order. You can create fun and tactile activities using a large wall or window because the material can slide around and is easily moved and rotated.

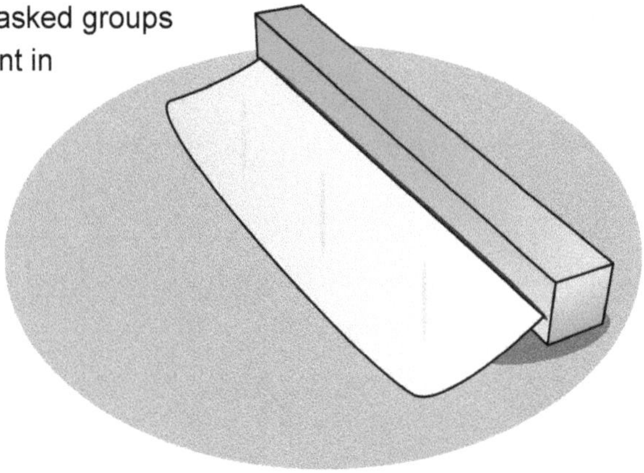

Tablecloths

The discovery of using tablecloths in team activities was transformative for me. It opened up so many new avenues of thought and enabled me to develop some powerful exercises. Disposable table cloths have important advantages over flipcharts: their size allows everybody to write on them at the same time and encourages the creation of much more ambitious visuals! A group working together around a table in this way is great for energy and engagement levels and promotes equal participation. The activity often becomes more creative as people approach the cloth from different angles and directions.

This probably goes without saying, but make sure you provide lots of different coloured pens to ensure the task has as much colour and creative potential as possible. A single tablecloth can normally allow a group of up to 8-10 people to work comfortably.

Look for high quality disposable paper table cloths – the various manufacturers typically use the term 'luxury tablecloths'. If you've never bought these before it's important to experiment with a few different options to find the best. The table cloth needs to be easy to write on with Sharpie style marker pens or felt tips, and it needs to be thick enough to prevent the ink bleeding through and marking the surface underneath. It is possible to buy wipe clean, disposable table cloths which have plastic on one side. These are ideal to use - just turn them upside down and write on the paper backing.

Spray mount

This is quite common in some European countries but seems to be less well known in the UK and USA. It is a light glue, similar in effect to the glue strip on a sticky note, which you spray directly onto any surface to make it lightly sticky. Once the surface has been sprayed, anything placed on that surface will stick but can also be peeled off and repositioned without losing its stickiness. To use this, you first need to cover a large enough surface with disposable paper - pin boards or whiteboards covered with large, cheap rolls of brown paper work well. It is also possible to use the spray mount on flipchart paper, but it can get a little messy since flipchart paper is smaller so it is harder to accurately spray only the intended surface!

There are a wide variety of applications for this product. You can ask groups to cut up magazines to create a collage (e.g. *"find images or headlines from a selection of magazines to summarise the key ideas from today/the culture of the team/the attitudes towards the finance department"* etc.). It also works effectively with call out cards, speech bubbles or index cards (all of which are normally purchased 'ready-made' in a variety of sizes and colours).

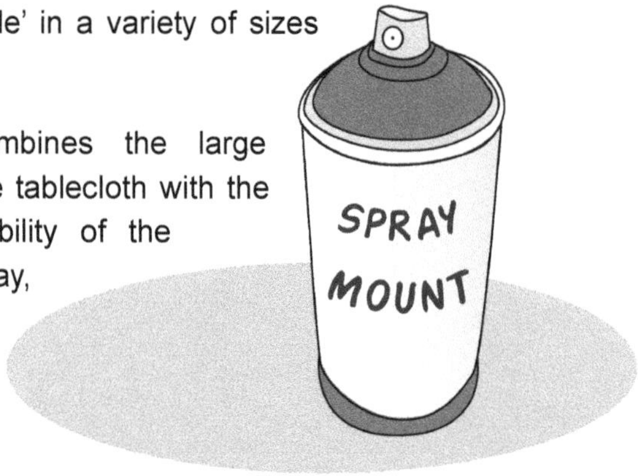

This technology combines the large creative canvas of the tablecloth with the interactivity and flexibility of the sticky note. In this way, activities designed around large boards with spray mount and call out cards are able to help people explore and process more complex information.

Large rolls of paper

To engage and tap into the creativity of an audience you need to provide a novel situation, context or environment. This is essentially what we have been exploring throughout this book. If you have a room with a large flat wall devoid of pictures, large joins, or features, then you could potentially use a large roll of paper. When I say large, I mean very large - floor to ceiling and wall to wall large!

I have used large rolls of paper for activities such as: Mapping exercises, flowcharts, strategy planning.

There is something incredibly powerful about seeing a huge blank sheet of paper taking form and filling up with the input of the audience. It is very satisfying at the end of the process to step back and see a clear visual. **There are two ways to facilitate using this technology:**

1. The facilitator allows the audience to stand up and work on the sheet all at the same time – this is high energy and unusual, and requires a lot of communication between participants to be successful.

2. The facilitator (or graphic illustrator, see later section) writes up on the page whilst the audience focuses on the discussion.

For mapping type activities, I normally allow the audience to write on the sheet. With strategic conversations, I throw a question out to the audience then I write down the key points of the conversation. Writing it all myself allows the audience to focus on their discussion and makes the finished page neater and easier to read.

Large rolls of paper can be purchased from paper supply companies. You will need a minimum of 2 metres in height and 3-4 metres in width minimum. The paper must have a high, thus heavy, GSM (grams per square metre). Test the paper with the pens you are going to use to ensure that the ink doesn't bleed through. Try holding the pen on the paper for a long time and with varying pressure. It would be embarrassing to take down the paper only to discover the wall behind has been marked by the writing.

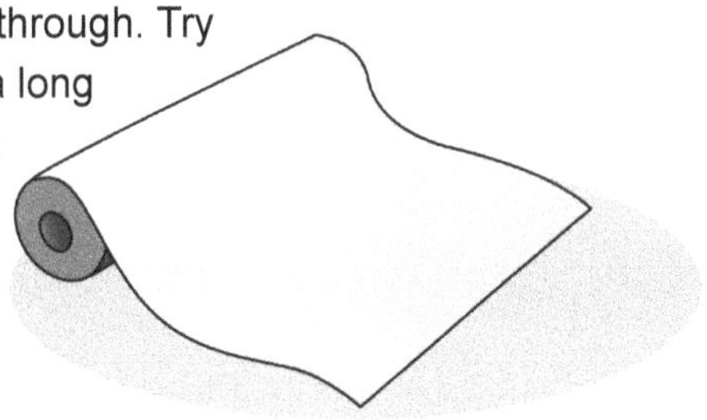

Alternatives to PowerPoint

Microsoft PowerPoint has long been the industry standard for electronic presentations but it is certainly not the only option. Other software packages and apps have successfully entered the market in recent years. The most interesting ones are those that challenge the very idea of 'a slide'. Packages that allow you to create and shape your communications in a different way will inspire you to find a new narrative style, and this novelty can be very refreshing for your audience.

There are new developments and software releases all the time but some current packages you might want to start with are:

- Prezi - www.prezi.com
- Slidedog - www.slidedog.com
- PowToon – www.powtoon.com
- SlideRocket - www.sliderocket.com

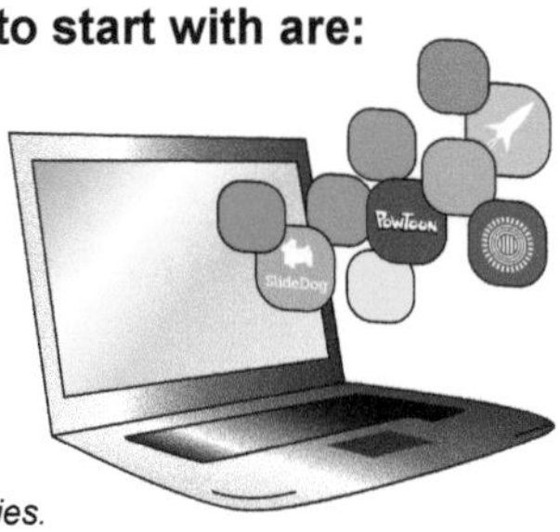

Microsoft and PowerPoint, are registered trademarks of Microsoft Corporation in the United States and/or other countries.

Interactive whiteboards (smartboards)

Interactive whiteboards were one of the most exciting technologies in this area some years ago. The most well-known brand is "SMART Board". It is essentially an electronic whiteboard and it operates in the same way. The board combines a projector with sensors to allow you to draw directly onto the screen using virtual pens. The end result is captured directly to your computer so it can be saved and sent out to participants after the session. To some extent the pace of technology has moved faster than the evolution of the boards. It is surprisingly rare to find a company that has invested in this technology and that uses it regularly. Even when this technology has been installed in a meeting room, few people seem to know how to use it.

Graphic illustrators

In fairness, this is more a person than a technology. Graphic illustrators or recorders can turn your conversations into wonderful visual images. Professional illustrators are a significant investment but well worth the time and money. A good illustrator will work creating images, whilst you hold the conversation with the group and will quickly create full page flipchart visualisations.

When selecting a graphic artist it is important to look beyond their drawing abilities. The most important quality in a good illustrator is the ability to interpret the conversation into images, analogies and metaphors. Dry topics can become dynamic, interesting, engaging and memorable. Long lists of key topics or action points can look more eye-catching and accessible.

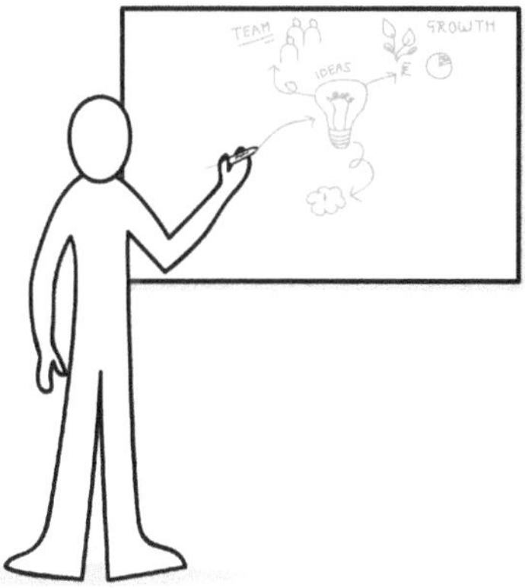

These visuals will not only wow your audience during an event but they are doubly valuable because they can be shared, printed and revisited by groups long after the event has finished. It is much easier to explain a strategy or concept based on a few good images rather than pages of typed text, meeting minutes, slides or flipcharts.

Scanner apps

When you are facilitating a session you often want to photograph to record and then circulate the work done in that session. There are various apps available which process and enhance your images to upgrade their quality. Typically these are described as 'scanner' apps and they will (if you photograph in good lighting) remove the background, leaving the text on a clean white background. This looks much more professional and the white background allows you to add them seamlessly into slides and documents. I use these apps for photographing all written work done during sessions; this includes flipcharts, tablecloths and the other creative technologies mentioned in this section. Experiment with the functionality of the app and learn how to capture the best images. You should also be prepared to physically move the subject matter around in order to get the best lighting on the surface you are photographing.

Generally this technology performs best when it is capturing text against a white background. Brightly coloured paper or sticky notes can affect the output quality of the image. However, 3M have created a wonderful app specifically for capturing sticky notes. Once you photograph your work, it recognises the shape of the individual notes and allows you to move them around onscreen as if they were real notes. Search for Post-it® Plus App[57].

Glass pens

Have you ever watched a television crime drama where the detectives stand in front of a sheet of glass and write up how the suspects are connected to the case? If you thought that looked quite cool or fun then I have exciting news, you too can write on glass using inexpensive glass-writing pens!

If you have meeting rooms with large glass windows this can be a simple and easy way to create unexpected and refreshing activities for your audience. Pens come in many different colours and thicknesses, so the end result can be visually striking. There is also something decidedly physical (connected to the multiple intelligences) about transforming the everyday transparent surface into a canvas for creativity.

In a similar vein, whiteboard or blackboard paint is available to transform walls into white or blackboard surfaces to write on. My experience with this technology is that the clean look on the first day quickly gives way to a smudged and discoloured surface. High quality paint and high quality cleaning fluids can reduce or delay this. For that reason, I prefer glass-writing pens. They clean completely and leave the surface unmarked even after multiple usage. One limitation to keep in mind is that it is unlikely you will be able to photograph your work. The experience is in the creativity and freedom; capturing the output directly is more challenging.

CHAPTER SUMMARY

SLIDES

Keep your slide design simple, use large font sizes and make them easy to understand within a few seconds. Try to use a minimal number of slides and include as many images as possible.

STICKY NOTES

Take the time to think about how to best use sticky notes. There are a surprising number of variables which can provide routes to creativity. Remember to peel off the notes sideways not bottom to top!

FLIPCHARTS

The same design rules for slides also apply here. Use large writing, lower case and try to avoid using joined-up handwriting. Use dark inks and only use red or green for accent colours, never for text.

For references and links from this chapter visit chris-atkinson.co.uk/books

VIDEOS

Videos can add great value to a presentation and can be informative or entertaining (or both!). You should however try to save the video to your computer so you are not relying on internet connection. Be cautious about using videos you find humorous.

GET CREATIVE

There are so many exciting and unusual things available for presenters and trainers to make their sessions more interactive and engaging. A simple stationery catalogue becomes a play-box of new ideas. Every month there are new apps and technologies that can be great fun to incorporate into a session.

7

COMPLETE REFERENCES

Now visit www.corporate-energy-book.com to discover free downloads to continue your learning.

1. http://www.aon.com/human-capital-consulting/thought-leadership/talent_mgmt/2014-trends-in-global-employee-engagement.jsp
2. http://dupress.com/periodical/trends/human-capital-trends-2015
3. http://www.nytimes.com/2003/12/14/magazine/14POWER.html
4. http://www.nytimes.com/2010/04/27/world/27powerpoint.html
5. http://archive.wired.com/wired/archive/11.09/ppt2.html
6. Lead From The Heart: Transformational Leadership For The 21st Century, Mark C. Crowley - ISBN-10: 145253540X ISBN-13: 978-1452535401 https://www.amazon.co.uk/Lead-Heart-Transformational-Leadership-Century/dp/145253540X
7. http://www.greatplacetowork.com/publications-and-events/publications/2185-become-best-places-to-work
8. Free Thinking: Purposeful Presentations by Martin Shovel http://www.trainingzone.co.uk/topic/soft-skills/free-thinking-purposeful-presentations
9. http://www.forbes.com/sites/nickmorgan/2011/02/02/243
10. http://www.duarte.com/presentation-organization-different-structures
11. http://www.speaklikeapro.co.uk/Structures.htm
12. https://en.wikipedia.org/wiki/Serial_position_effect
13. https://en.wikipedia.org/wiki/Hermann_Ebbinghaus
14. http://www.simplypsychology.org/primacy-recency.html

15. https://en.wikipedia.org/wiki/First_impression_(psychology)

16. Teach Yourself Presenting, Amanda Vickers and Steve Bavister - ISBN-10: 0340941758 ISBN-13: 978-0340941751 http://www.amazon.co.uk/Teach-Yourself-Presenting-Steve-Bavister/dp/0340941758

17. http://news.bbc.co.uk/1/hi/magazine/3993483.stm

18. https://en.wikipedia.org/wiki/Albert_Mehrabian

19. The Man Who Mistook his Wife for a Hat, Oliver Sacks - ISBN-10: 0330523627 ISBN-13: 978-0330523622 https://www.amazon.co.uk/Man-Who-Mistook-His-Wife/dp/0330523627

20. http://www.forbes.com/sites/carminegallo/2012/09/06/7-sure-fire-ways-great-leaders-inspire-people-to-follow-them

21. https://hbr.org/2011/04/boost-power-through-body-langu.html

22. http://hbswk.hbs.edu/item/power-posing-fake-it-until-you-make-it

23. http://www.amazon.com/The-Definitive-Book-Body-Language/dp/0553804723

24. https://q12.gallup.com

25. http://www.wilmarschaufeli.nl/downloads/test-manuals

26. http://www.gallup.com/services/178514/state-american-workplace.aspx

27. http://www.gallup.com/services/178517/state-global-workplace.aspx

28. http://www.gallup.com/poll/165269/worldwide-employees-engaged-work.aspx

29. http://www.economistinsights.com/leadership-talent-innovation/analysis/re-engaging-engagement

30. How to Win Friends and Influence People, Dale Carnegie - ISBN-10: 0091906814 ISBN-13: 978-0091906818 https://www.amazon.co.uk/How-Win-Friends-Influence-People/dp/0091906814

31. https://en.wikipedia.org/wiki/Neuro-linguistic_programming

32. https://en.wikipedia.org/wiki/Showmanship_(performing)

33. http://workplacepsychology.net/2010/06/11/leadership-southwest-airlines-malice-in-dallas

34. https://en.wikipedia.org/wiki/Bloom%27s_taxonomy

35. https://en.wikipedia.org/wiki/Neuro-linguistic_programming

36. Modeling with NLP, Robert D. Dilts - ISBN-10: 091699046X ISBN-13: 978-0916990466 https://www.amazon.co.uk/Modeling-NLP-Robert-D-Dilts/dp/091699046X

37. http://www.leadershipchallenge.com

38. http://blogs.hbr.org/cs/2012/08/are_you_sure_youre_not_a_bad_b.html

39. http://blogs.hbr.org/2013/10/leaders-drop-your-masks

40. https://hbr.org/2005/12/managing-authenticity-the-paradox-of-great-leadership

41. https://www.ted.com/talks/brene_brown_on_vulnerability?language=en

42. http://howardgardner.com/books

43. Wired to Care: How Companies Prosper When They Create Widespread Empathy, Dev Patnaik - ISBN-10: 013714234X ISBN-13: 978-0137142347 https://www.amazon.co.uk/Wired-Care-Companies-Prosper-Widespread/dp/013714234X http://www.wiredtocare.com

44. http://harari.blogspot.co.uk

45. Collins, J.C. & Porras, J.I. (1996). Building your company's vision. Harvard Business Review https://hbr.org/1996/09/building-your-companys-vision

46. https://en.wikipedia.org/wiki/Ironic_process_theory

47. Winter Notes on Summer Impressions, Fyodor Dostoevsky - ISBN-10: 1847490646 ISBN-13: 978-1847490643 https://www.amazon.co.uk/Winter-Summer-Impressions-Oneworld-Classics/dp/1847490646

48. http://www.businessinsider.com/we-believe-that-were-on-the-face-of-the-earth-to-make-great-products-and-thats-not-2011-1?IR=T

49. https://hbr.org/1996/09/building-your-companys-vision

50. The Road Less Travelled (Arrow New-Age), M. Scott Peck - ISBN-10: 0099727404 ISBN-13: 978-0099727408 https://www.amazon.co.uk/Road-Less-Travelled-Arrow-New-Age/dp/0099727404 https://en.wikipedia.org/wiki/M._Scott_Peck

51. Business Beyond the Box: Applying Your Mind for Breakthrough Results, John O'Keeffe - ISBN-10: 185788213X ISBN-13: 978-1857882131 https://www.amazon.co.uk/Business-Beyond-Box-Applying-Breakthrough/dp/185788213X https://books.google.co.uk/books?isbn=1857884787

52. https://en.wikipedia.org/wiki/Pareto_principle

53. Edward Tufte - https://www.edwardtufte.com/tufte/powerpoint

54. http://www.amazon.co.uk/Learning-Science-Instruction-Guidelines-Multimedia/dp/0787986836

55. https://en.wikipedia.org/wiki/Flipped_classroom

56. http://www.pechakutcha.org

57. http://www.post-it.com/3M/en_US/post-it/ideas/plus-app

WHAT NEXT?

Now that you have read the book, the first challenge is to ensure that you PRACTISE the techniques. I have emphasised throughout the book that the skills and suggestions may not feel right first time nor are they any guarantee of immediate success. It will take practice, perseverance, support and encouragement. Make sure you have people around you who will be honest and let you know when you do things that work well. It takes a lot of courage to admit to people that you are trying something new; most leaders and managers are stuck in patterns of behaviour which hardly change over their entire career.

The second challenge is get EXPERIMENTAL and CREATIVE. The likelihood is that when applying the ideas from the book, you chose relatively safe options, but I'm certain that as you were reading some elements felt more challenging or risky. Once you have seen successes from the safer options, push yourself to try something a little bolder, experiment with some of the more creative ideas. In this way you will surprise your audience who will not expect that from you. Doing something unexpected is an easy way to grab attention!

Thirdly, please VISIT THE WEBSITE (www.corporate-energy-book.com) as it is an integral part of this book. It is filled with additional downloads, articles, videos and new ideas. In addition, all of the references in the book are listed by number on the website. This is so that we can ensure all of the links are up to date and you can click straight through to the relevant reference or article.

Finally, these skills and techniques are learnt fastest through application with a professional coach. There are four COURSES available which are all based on the content of this book. These programmes are all one or two days long and can be delivered anywhere in the world. If you are interested in any of these programmes, please visit the website to find out more or e-mail info@chris-atkinson.co.uk

Connecting with Chris

My fundamental belief is that work isn't the problem here. This isn't about the nature of work itself. It would be easy for people to say, "I work in this industry..." or, "I do this type of work, so how am I going to find pleasure, inspiration or engagement?" I don't believe it's possible for everyone to bounce in to work every day. But I do believe that it is an issue of corporate culture and attitude. I've seen individuals and teams find pleasure and satisfaction - even excitement - in the most challenging and the most seemingly monotonous roles.

I've worked with a lot of people over many years. When I reflect on all of those people, I wonder how many truly felt passion for their work or even enjoyed it - as a minimum standard. Even if we estimate that fifty percent of people enjoy their job, which I believe is probably significantly too high, it is still a horrifying thought. Picture these people - your teams, your colleagues - in their offices all day, doing something that isn't satisfying them, not enriching their life in some way. To me, that is worrying and it feels dysfunctional.

Consequently, the impact I hope to make in the world is:

I want to help people connect with a passion for their working life and for working with others!

Here are two powerful ways you can work with Chris:

Speaking

If you would like Chris to speak at a corporate event or run a seminar tailored specifically for your organisation or audience, please contact him on **info@chris-atkinson.co.uk**

Voluntary work

In addition to his speaking work, Chris reserves a number of days each year to support charities and voluntary organisations worldwide at no cost. To explore how he could work with you in this way, find out more at **www.chris-atkinson.co.uk/charity**

Programmes based on the book

The following programmes are designed to bring the material from the book to LIFE! They are the next step in the process of improving your professional impact and influence through communication.

Theory is not enough, most of us learn by doing! All of the following programmes are suitable for 6-12 people and can be delivered bespoke for your organisational context.

The courses listed over the next few pages can be run face to face, anywhere in the world. The delivery team are dynanic trainers and facilitators, who embody the best practice principles detailed in this book. You will see the concepts in action and be personally challenged to communicate with greater impact. The programmes are practical, packed with new ideas and delivered by world class trainers.

We also have a selection of alternative versions of the content available as:

- Webinars
- Online learning
- Train the trainer

Want to find to find out more? Get in touch:

chris-atkinson.co.uk

info@chris-atkinson.co.uk

Find the core programmes listed on the next few pages...

CORPORATE ENERGY TRAINING

2 Days

"Learn the skills needed to entertain an audience whilst taking their active engagement to a new level! Leave the course invigorated, confident, full of new ideas and impatient to get back to work to try it all out!"

Culturally, business has become dominated with long meetings, dry content driven training sessions and dull PowerPoint presentations. These have the impact of 'sucking' energy from our people, breaking down relationships and destroying productivity.

The 2-day Corporate Energy programme is an interactive highly challenging programme. All participants are required to develop their own material in the sessions and are then individually coached whilst delivering it. The combination of live presenting, feedback and refined practice, allows you to hone this skill set in front of 'safe audience', in a positive environment.

The programme teaches participants how to make sure the presenter stays the focus for the audience (not slides), how to energise audiences while learning to balance entertainment with content delivery. Other important skills learnt range from storytelling, showmanship, facilitation skills and how to respond to hostile audiences.

INSIDE INSPIRATION - INSPIRE OTHERS

1 Day

"Tap into a new emotional communication style by revealing more of yourself. Creates a more authentic, persuasive, compelling presence in front of audiences"

After many years of hearing people say they'd like to be more inspirational or charismatic, I realised this is an area that is not really tackled within organisations. The cost of ignoring this issue is huge, research has shown that 'being inspirational' is one of the critical traits that elevates leaders into achieving extraordinary performance from their teams. Simply put, inspiration is a product of authenticity, how genuine we are when we speak and how much comes from the heart. For that reason, it is a skill that can be learnt - but it requires a safe environment, honest feedback and someone to challenge you.

Participants on this programme learn key strategies to speak with more emotion. Harnessing emotion can help you reveal a new leadership style that builds trust with your audience. This programme provides many opportunities to practise. Practicing a wide range of techniques in a safe environment allows the participant to gauge and refine the effectiveness of their communication style. Become a more influential communicator, enhance your career, relationships with colleagues and your team working. Make an impact!

corporate-energy-book.com/programmes/

FANTASTIC FACILITATION

1 or 2 Day

"The skills of effective facilitation are now essential for all business professionals. Learn the secrets to engaging people and eliciting their input in a focussed way."

The negative impact of many dull and lifeless conversations in business has led to a demand to engage audiences effectively. This programme gives you a complete toolkit to create innovative and engaging ways to discuss information. Learn the critical communication skills of a facilitator and how to handle the pressure of leading conversations.

Learn the art of audience-led facilitation and how to shift communication from 'tell' to 'ask'. Practice using a facilitation style that allows you to approach ANY subject with confidence regardless of your expertise in that area. By utilising the expertise of the people in the room, you do not need to be an expert and can stay focused on guiding the dialogue, keeping it on track. You will find this new level of flexibility can be transferred into all professional circumstances enabling you to effectively question and lead conversations in a strong assertive manner. The outcome is focused productive interactions where the participants are contributing and motivated.

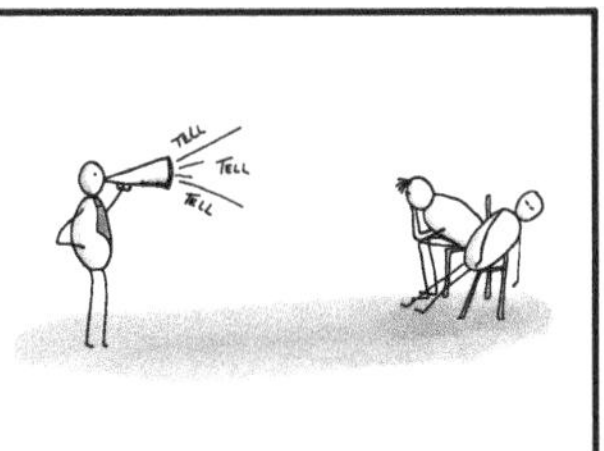

GO FROM ONE WAY COMMUNICATION TO FACILITATING A DIALOGUE BETWEEN YOU & THE AUDIENCE...

CREATE A COLLABORATIVE CULTURE WHERE PEOPLE CAN BE INVOLVED & MAKE A DIFFERENCE...

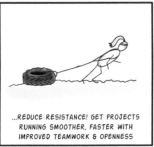

...REDUCE RESISTANCE! GET PROJECTS RUNNING SMOOTHER, FASTER WITH IMPROVED TEAMWORK & OPENNESS

...USE THE EXPERTISE IN THE ROOM - YOU DON'T NEED TO BE AN EXPERT. GUIDE CONVERSATIONS IN THE RIGHT DIRECTION

corporate-energy-book.com/programmes/

BEYOND PRESENTATION SKILLS - CREATING A STRATEGIC LEADERSHIP NARRATIVE

2 Days

"This programme will challenge and push even the most skilful of presenters to raise their ability. Leave with the skills to transform your commercial communications!"

There is a strong movement in leadership now, towards creating a narrative in the structure of business presentations that sells the commercial context to the audience without the typical 'weight' of normal management presentations. Using techniques such as storytelling, analogy, evidence, personal examples and humour we can create more memorable and impactful presentations. In addition, by revealing more of our personal passion, conviction and belief we become more charismatic and inspiring.

This programme is delivered by two trainers, using a video camera to film your presentations and private 1:1 coaching. More than 50% of the programme is dedicated to practice, giving you the opportunity to try out techniques in a safe environment so that you can get comfortable and confident with your enhanced skills. The practice exercises are coached intensively and recorded for private review to reinforce retention and application of the learned skills.

CREATE A NARRATIVE THAT SELLS COMMERCIAL CONTEXT..
TRANSFORM DRY CONTENT. FULLY ENGAGE YOUR AUDIENCE...
...GET PRIVATE 1:1 COACHING THROUGHOUT YOUR PRACTICE. REVIEW FILMS OF YOURSELF TO HELP REINFORCE LEARNING
...TAKE YOUR SKILLS TO THE NEXT LEVEL. TRULY TRANSFORM YOUR CORPORATE COMMUNICATION

CPSIA information can be obtained
at www.ICGtesting.com
Printed in the USA
LVHW052050100619
620694LV00011B/330/P

9 781911 079415